ENVIRONMENTS FOR LEARNING

ENVIRONMENTS FOR LEARNING

Eric Jensen

with

Michael Dabney
Karen Markowitz
Karen Selsor

THE BRAIN STORE
Resources for Growing Minds ®

Environments for Learning

Eric Jensen

 ©2003 The Brain Store®

Contributing Writers: Michael Dabney • Karen Markowitz • Karen Selsor
Designer: Tracy Linares
Developmental/Managing Editor: Karen Markowitz
Cover Photo Courtesy of SHW Group, Inc., McKinney ISD

Printed in the United States of America
Published by The Brain Store®
San Diego, CA, USA

ISBN #1-890460-24-9

Library of Congress Cataloging-in-Publication Data

Jensen, Eric
Environments for Learning
Includes biographical references and index.
ISBN:1-890460-24-9
I. Education—Teaching.

For additional copies or bulk discounts contact:

The Brain Store®
4202 Sorrento Valley Blvd., Ste. B • San Diego, CA 92121
Phone (858) 546-7555 • Fax (858) 546-7560 • www.thebrainstore.com

Environments are the medium in which we live. We can feel them everyday, all day long. At school only the quality of the teacher is a greater determinant of student success than the environment. One environment brings out the best in us and another brings out the worst in us. They can be nourishing or toxic, supportive or draining. Environments are never neutral. How important are they? How important is water to fish?

—Eric Jensen

Table of Contents

1

What Students Feel

2

What Students See

3

What Students Hear

4
What Students Smell, Taste, and Breathe

5
The Total Environment

Appendix

Introduction

The first thing we do when we walk into any new space, whether
consciously or unconsciously, is look around, listen, breathe, and
form judgments about the environment. We decide whether it's
familiar, safe, friendly, or not. This automatic filtering of environmental cues is an ongoing process that occurs every minute of
every hour we are awake. It is so much a part of being human that
most of us don't give it a second thought. However, when it comes
to creating the optimal educational environment, we can learn a
lot by giving a second thought to what students see, hear, feel,
smell, breathe, and taste in the places dedicated to their learning.

A good deal of research has been conducted on environments
lately—much of it centered on the phrase "enriched environments." This term refers to specially orchestrated environments
for learning; it encompasses the students, teachers, and activities
that contribute to the total learning context. Here, we've nar-
rowed the focus to the physical environment of the classroom.
The "interactive" (or relational) aspect of environments (including enrichment) will be addressed in a separate minibook. In
short, our focus here is what educators can *do to* the environment
before students even arrive.

To the extent possible, the physical environment of an optimal
classroom is aesthetically pleasant, attractive, colorful, comfortable, and engaging to the senses. Since the environment is a variable that can be easily enhanced, it makes good sense for teachers

to take full advantage of it. Students ought to be provided with an almost constant opportunity for sensory stimulation—things to hear, touch, see and smell—up to many times the amount of material conventionally introduced in traditional classrooms.

Maximum attention ought to be given to creating an engaging, interesting, and safe environment. In such a setting, students unconsciously begin to acquire a foundation for "understanding" before they even know they know something; in fact, even before the teacher enters the room.

This practical research-based resource aims to present the bottom line, the core, the guts of what we know and can do to optimize achievement by attending to learners' inner and outer worlds.

1 — *What Students Feel*

Safety, Safety, Safety

Not surprisingly, the brain devotes much of its resources to ensuring our survival. Our brain is always tracking how we feel, what the environment feels like, and our sense of touch. Some 30 million bits per second of information are processed nonconsciously in our tactile sensory areas. As humans, we are exquisitely designed to be sensitive to our environment. Therefore, we can make a huge difference in our classrooms by realizing the importance of tending to physical and emotional climate with careful planning and a heightened awareness of the importance of student comfort and safety.

As the problem of school violence and accompanying measures to prevent it (armed security guards, security checkpoints, locked doors) become ever more prevalent in the lives of many children, school officials are increasingly concerned about the effect this change in environment is having on the learning process.

Recent studies suggest that, whether perceived or real, the threat of violence in the learning environment can have a negative impact on cognition. Specifically, the stress associated with violence impacts test scores, absenteeism, tardiness, and attention span (Hoffman 1996).

Scientists know that the learning brain does not respond well to real or imagined threats of harm. Such environments trigger the amygdala (the brain's fear and emotional response center) to release an overabundance of cortisol and adrenaline. When the stress state is triggered, the body goes into "fight or flight" mode: its first and sole priority is to ward off danger. This state, when chronic, shuts down formal learning.

In a study of 35 fourth graders and 39 fifth graders, Nettles and colleagues (2000) concluded that children's perceived exposure to violence negatively affects test scores. It was found that students who perceived their environment to be violent performed significantly lower on standardized exams of reading and mathematics compared to students who did not have a perceived exposure to violence.

Citing a 1994 Roper Poll, the researchers report that more than 10% of high-school students stayed home or skipped classes due to fear of violence. The poll also cited that 160,000 children occasionally miss school because of intimidation or fear of bodily harm. Evidence also suggests that kids who are afraid to walk home from school because of neighborhood bullies, gang intimidation, drive-by shootings, and other threats may be less likely to participate in sports and other after-school activities. Other figures cited by Smith and Feiler (1995) are equally disturbing because they indicate the problem is not just relegated to the inner city. Twenty percent of suburban high-school students surveyed in 1995 endorsed shooting someone "who has stolen something from you," and 8% believed it okay to shoot a person "who had done something to offend or insult you."

Strategies You Can Use

- Discuss the threat of school violence (whether perceived or real) openly with your students. Let them air their fears and anxieties about the situation. Divide the class into small groups to discuss ways in which students can prevent school violence.
- Adopt a zero tolerance policy towards bullying. Let students know they are safe.
- Encourage school administrators and security personnel to form supportive alliances with parents and neighborhood groups.
- Seek the advice of other professionals as needed, including the school psychologist.
- Teach emotional intelligence skills.
- Make the room inviting to students; use music, flowers, warm colors, and affirming posters.

- Maintain a caring attitude that is accepting of diversity: culture, gender, race, class, lifestyle.
- Role model positive ways to deal with temporary setbacks, mistakes, and challenges. Laugh at yourself when you make a minor mistake, for example. Show students that it is okay to be wrong sometimes; that it's part of learning.

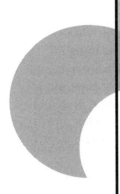

Bottom Line

Above all else, physical safety is a primary consideration for teachers. Each teacher should be familiar with how to effectively respond to various emergency situations. Teachers must know where the fire extinguisher is and the nearest phone. In addition, keep a current list of parents, doctors, and emergency phone numbers close by and a first-aid kit with plenty of gauze, tape, and Band-Aids. Also keep a broom accessible for cleaning up broken glass and rags available for messy clean ups. Know how to contact the custodial department if necessary. Other necessities include knowing emergency procedures for fires, earthquakes, floods, hurricanes, explosions, power failures, and blizzards. The overall safety of students is just as important as the other things teachers do each day.

Ergonomics and Cognition

How might the design of students' desks play a role in their cognition? More than you probably realize, says Galen Cranz (1998), professor of architecture at the University of California, Berkeley. Dr. Cranz calls for a more pragmatic and posture-friendly approach to the way we design and use chairs—from the boardroom to the classroom.

The traditional classroom desk pushes the sitter's weight straight down, increasing pressure on the lower back and forcing students to sit *on* the chair rather than *in* it. Warning against equating cushiness with comfort, Cranz proposes that a good classroom desk keeps the shoulders back and the chin up, as well as provides arm rests to minimize strain on the upper body. In addition, she says, a good chair should have as much adjustability as possible and be easy to modify. The seat should not be so long that it digs into the back of the legs, nor should it be so high that feet don't touch the floor.

Best Chair Design for Learning
✔ Rounded front edge so that circulation is not cut off in the thighs
✔ Angled writing surface to ease eye strain while reading
✔ Small-back support that can be adjusted for a good fit
✔ Foot rest to improve circulation

The further off chairs are from this ideal seat design, the more it makes sense to get students up and moving more often.

Research suggests that the chair can be a crucial factor in preventing adverse health and cognitive effects. An effectively designed chair can also help improve learner and employee performance. Conversely, scientists know that ill-supportive chairs prevent the nervous system and the disks in the vertebra area from receiving direct blood supply. This causes fatigue and eventually back pain or discomfort, which impede cognition (Linton, et al. 1994; Mark, et al. 1991).

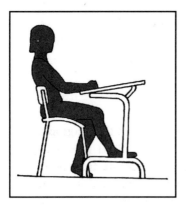

The need for more ergonomically enhanced classroom seating is even more important as students (from elementary school on) spend increasing amounts of time at the computer in chairs with little or no support. As a result, more and more students are developing back problems in their 20s, Linton and colleagues (1994) report. Linton's 1994 study involving three classes of fourth-graders found that the introduction of ergonomically designed school furniture resulted in a significant reduction in musculoskeletal symptoms among students. Back pain is second only to the common cold as a reason given by adults for missing work, costing an estimated 70 billion dollars annually (Cranz 1998).

Seating for Success

Can students concentrate more effectively sitting in rows rather than around a table or in small groups? As you might have guessed, it depends on the particular task and the prevalence of behavioral and learning difficulties in the classroom (Hastings 2000). Among students with behavioral and moderate learning problems, one study suggests a highly structured seating arrangement tends to be more effective (Wheldall & Lam, 1987). Their study of 34 special-education students (ages 12 - 25) concluded that on-task behavior doubled from 35 to 70% when seating was changed from tables to rows. In addition, the rate of classroom disruption by the students was three times higher at tables (ibid).

Other research suggests that while group seating can foster important social and peer interaction among students, such arrangements often produce an increase in chatting and other disturbances that discourage deep concentration (Bennett & Blundell 1983). Conversely, row seating provides a more structured setting, allowing students to focus more on the task at hand rather than on each other. This does not imply that group or table-seating arrangements should be eliminated completely, but rather used judiciously, researchers emphasize. In fact, the *integration* of group activities with traditional learning tasks has been found to have *a significant positive impact* on learning.

Previous research by Hastings (1995) produced similar findings: group seating around tables with four or more makes learning more difficult for the most distractible pupils. One portion of the study found that on-task time dramatically increased when row seating was instituted, but group seating was more conducive to genuinely cooperative learning. The impact of group seating on team learning was also borne out in a study by Marx and colleagues (1999), who found that fourth-graders tended to ask more questions *when seated in a semicircle* than in a row-and-column arrangement. This finding supports prior studies and bears out the benefit of cluster seating for group discussions and interactive learning tasks. The key, therefore, is to match the appropriate seating arrangement to the activity—for example, using a cluster arrangement when collaboration is the goal or row seating when concentrated independent learning is the goal.

Cognitive scientists know that during intense mental activity, the brain benefits from a structured learning environment, especially one that is devoid of distractions. The brain cannot concentrate well on more than one stimulus at a time. Distractions (no matter how benign) force various brain regions, including the frontal lobes, which control willpower, concentration, planning, and other executive functions, to compete between multiple stimuli. This increases the potential for errors and can reduce work speed and quality.

Strategies You Can Use

- Unattached chairs and moveable desks are best for maximum seating comfort and flexibility.
- Provide regular brief breaks (every 10-15 minutes); facilitate a movement activity (i.e., stretching, breathing, cross-lateral movments) to "wake up" the brain and nervous system.
- Give students the liberty to position themselves in flexible ways. For example, allow them to lean up against a wall or sit on the floor while reading. Or, allow students to find a friend to "pair-share" with while walking (roller-derby style) around the room.
- Ask students to stand occasionally for brief learning periods—for example, while you conduct a review or facilitate a partner exchange.
- Encourage your school (or management) to investigate the possibility of acquiring ergonomically correct chairs, desks, and computer stations for students and workers.
- Encourage learners and workers not to slump while sitting, as it over stretches the muscles and ligaments and puts undue stress on the back. In addition, poor posture shifts the body out of balance and forces a few muscles and joints to do all the work.
- Poor physical conditioning, like poor posture, also plays a role in back pain and fatigue. When appropriate, encourage learners and workers to incorporate movement and exercise into their daily routines.
- Remain flexible about the seating arrangements in your classroom. Row seating tends to provide better support and structure for classroom work requiring an internal focus (i.e., writing, content delivery, etc.), while cluster seating tends to foster interaction, teamwork, and the generation of ideas.
- If you use group seating routinely for all types of class work, place no more than two or three students together at a table and refrain from placing friends in the same group. This may help reduce the incidence of idle chitchat and distractions.

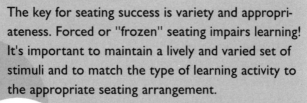

Bottom Line

The key for seating success is variety and appropriateness. Forced or "frozen" seating impairs learning! It's important to maintain a lively and varied set of stimuli and to match the type of learning activity to the appropriate seating arrangement.

Where a student sits in class affects his or her learning experiences, so provide some flexibility. Students remain more alert and focused when given a choice of seating arrangement (floor or chair) and permission to stand or walk around if desired. Remind students that the room looks different from various angles; that they can gain additional insights and experiences by changing vantage points. Switching seats can give students a fresh perspective and provide the impetus for leaving outdated limiting patterns behind.

Classroom Size Does Matter

Although the issue of class size is still debatable (and probably will be for some time), research does suggest that smaller class sizes can have a significant and positive impact on learning and teacher interaction. Studies reveal that smaller classes can increase individual instruction time in grades K through 12; increase early learning and cognitive skills in preschoolers; and enhance reading and mathematics performance in elementary students, especially among educationally disadvantaged children (Betts & Shkolnik 1999; Bosker 1997; Finn, et al. 1990; Mosteller 1995).

Scientists know the brain responds exceptionally well to learning environments with high levels of individualized instruction, constructive feedback, small-group interaction, and high expectations—elements that have been shown to occur more readily in smaller classrooms (Sommers 1990). Research conducted by Frank and Greenberg (1994) and others indicates that such enriched settings facilitate thinking and learning by strengthening important neural connections that aid long-term memory, planning, and decision-making. This process is especially important in the brain development of young children.

Most interesting is that the cognitive benefits of small class interaction can be lasting ones. In a four-year study of class size on the short- and long-term academic performance of 6,500 elementary students in 330 classrooms, Mosteller (1995) found that improvements in math and reading realized during the study continued for months after. In fact, by the end of the study, students in 17 of the most economically disadvantaged schools had improved their standing in reading and math from well below-average to above-average, Mosteller reports.

Large classes tend to generate more "safety" and "threat" concerns, which ultimately impact cognition. The larger the group, the more social-status groupings tend to be formed, which influence serotonin and cortisol levels. Generally, when we feel safe we have a higher serotonin level; when we feel unsafe or stressed we have a higher cortisol level. Chronically high cortisol levels are bad for the body and learning.

Researchers suggest that the optimal class size for grades K through 12 is 21 or fewer students. A class with 22 to 27 students is considered of moderate size, while one with 27 to 34 is considered large. A class with more than 35 students is detrimental to academic achievement, according to studies by Bosker (1997) and Sommers (1990).

Strategies You Can Use

- Regularly incorporate small-group learning activities (led by either teacher or students or a combination of both).
- Experiment with seating and desk arrangements. For example, a more personal setting can be created by moving desks in a circle or along the walls with the center open for student and teacher interaction.
- A change of venue can personalize the experience of learning in a large group. For example, you might occasionally hold a meaningful lesson outside in a comfortable area (i.e., nearby park or grass field).

Temperature Is Critical

One of the first things a person notices when entering a room is the temperature; this is a consideration often overlooked by teachers. Yet we know that the human brain is extremely temperature sensitive—a factor that significantly impacts cognition. In U.S. Defense Department studies, Taylor and Orlansky (1993) reported that heat stress dramatically lowered scores in both intellectual and physical tasks. Jeffrey Lackney (1994) at the University of Wisconsin, Madison has shown that reading comprehension declines when room temperature rises above 74 degrees Fahrenheit while math skills decline above 77 degrees Fahrenheit.

Up to a point, the cooler your brain is, the more relaxed, receptive, and cognitively sharp you are. Generally, cooler (not cold) is better than warmer (or hot). Our body, for example, can adjust to a room that is 5 degrees too cold better than one that is five degrees too hot. However, classrooms kept between 68 and 72 degrees Fahrenheit are most comfortable for the majority of students (Harner 1974). Harner reports that an ambient temperature of approximately 70 degrees is ideal for most learning situations, particularly those involving reading and mathematics, in which optimal focus and concentration is required.

Researchers report that higher temperatures can influence neurotransmitter levels—especially norepinephrine and serotonin, two chemicals associated with moods ranging from depression to relaxation (Donovan, et al. 1999; Howard 1994; Izard, et al. 1984). Excess levels of neurotransmitters can lead to aggressive behavior—a persistent obstacle to learning. This basic insight sheds light on the important role temperature plays in the learning environment, and how it can affect our behavior, thoughts, and emotions.

Other findings on temperature and cognition include the following:

✔ Hot, humid weather was linked to increased episodes of panic attacks in an empirical study involving 154 patients at the Montefiore Medical Center in New York (Asnis 1999).
✔ A significant increase in body temperature in children with Attention-Deficit/Hyperactivity Disorder can lead to increased aggressiveness, especially when the serotonin-enhancing drug d,l-fenfluramine (FEN) is administered (Donovan, et al. 1999).
✔ An empirical study suggests a link between high incidences of suicide and severe depression among the elderly during the summer months of June and July (Salib 1997).

It is important that teachers remember to attend to temperature matters—an easy thing to forget once engrossed in the multiple tasks at hand. When you enter or leave the room, make a habit of consciously checking the temperature gauge. Also consider whether the air is stagnant or circulating. If necessary, open windows and doors. For teachers who are interested and have access to them, ionizers and humidifiers can increase classroom comfort in dry weather. About 20% of the population are adversely affected by atmospheric electrical charges, which occur particularly when the weather turns super dry and static electricity is prevalent. A negative ionizer can counteract these effects.

Strategies You Can Use

- Consider the following alternatives if you don't have a temperature control in your classroom: (1) use fans; (2) keep windows or doors open; (3) point fans across a tray of water to humidify or cool; (4) allow students to move around to cooler or shaded areas; (5) incorporate colors that create cooling effects, such as blues and greens; (6) encourage students to layer clothing for more flexibility; and (7) ensure students hydrate often.
- When relaxation is required, keep temperature in the upper range of the comfort zone (70-72 degrees).
- When alertness is desired, keep temperature in the lower range of the comfort zone (68-70 degrees).
- When planning and conducting sessions with the elderly, be aware of their heightened sensitivity to cool temperatures. And in sessions involving individuals with such conditions as panic disorder or Attention-Deficit/Hyperactivity Disorder, be mindful of how extremely warm temperatures can increase anxiety or aggressiveness.
- Many teachers have found it helpful to attach a ribbon next to a window or air conditioner so that they can tell if the air is circulating.

Bottom Line

Classroom temperature is often overlooked and is an essential element for establishing a comfortable learning environment. Rooms kept between 68 and 72 degrees Fahrenheit are most comfortable for the majority of students. Provide good air circulation by opening windows and doors if weather permits. School buildings with central temperature controls can be very frustrating for teachers. We expect teachers to work miracles with students each day, yet they may not even have control over the most basic environmental conditions.

2   *What Students See*

Lighting and Learning

Early school starting times have students spending more time in darker environments. Lifestyle and safety concerns mean fewer children walk to school. Budget constraints and apathy frequently result in less than adequate school lighting. And lack of awareness continues the under-utilization of natural lighting. In fact, some children spend six continuous hours or more in school facilities illuminated by artificial light. But is this really a problem? It could be, says Dr. Jacob Liberman, author of *Light: Medicine of the Future* (1991).

Liberman points out that over the past 100 years, the amount of outdoor light we are generally exposed to has declined. Ultraviolet light, present only outdoors, activates the synthesis of vitamin D, which aids in the absorption of essential minerals such as calcium (MacLaughlin, et al. 1982). And, insufficient mineral intake has been shown to be a con-

tributing factor in nonverbal cognitive deficiency, report Benton and Roberts (1988).

Even early on, a very large blind study examined the impact of environmental factors on learning problems and reported that more than 50% of children developed academic or health deficiencies as a result of insufficient light at school (Harmon 1951). The study, which evaluated 160,000 school children, also reported that when lighting was improved, the following problems were dramatically reduced, as depicted by the chart on the next page:

Problem	Percent Reduction
visual difficulties	*65 %*
nutritional deficits	*48 %*
chronic infections	*43 %*
postural problems	*26 %*
chronic fatigue	*56 %*

Another more recent study conducted by the Heschong Mahone Consulting Group in California (unpublished: 1999) studied 21,000 students from three districts in three states. After reviewing school facilities, architectural plans, aerial photographs, and maintenance plans, each classroom was assigned a code indicating the amount of sunlight it received during particular times of the day and year. Controlling for variables, the study found that students with the most sunlight in their classrooms progressed 20% faster on math tests and 26% faster on reading tests compared to students with the least lighting.

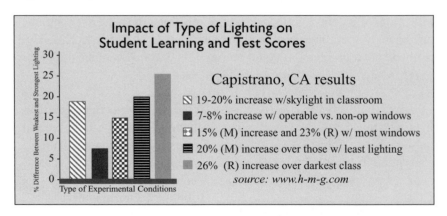

Since many bodily functions and hormones are regulated by daily dark-light cycles, it is not surprising that a link has been established between seasonal mood changes and amount of light present during the day (Brennan, et al. 1999; Sher, et al. 1999). Scientists know that limited exposure to sunlight for extended periods suppresses the production of melatonin, a neurotransmitter that plays a key role in setting the body's time clock or circadian rhythm. Beyond this, too little sunlight also decreases the production of serotonin, which at reduced levels causes depression. Ultimately, mood, alertness, and cognitive performance are compromised as a result (Antoniadis, et al. 2000).

Chronic and intense mood changes that include depression during winter months may be a sign of Seasonal Affective Disorder (SAD). Estimates are that 5% of school-age children are depressed. But exposure to bright lighting for extended periods can reduce the symptoms (Yamada, et al. 1995). Studies by Schwartz and colleagues (1998) confirm the key roles that melatonin and serotonin play in SAD.

Bright Lighting Increases Alertness

Why is bright light in the classroom and work environment so conducive to alertness? Scientists know that darkness triggers the release of melatonin, a sleep-producing hormone excreted by the pineal gland in the brain. Conversely, bright light tends to slow or prevent the production of melatonin, thereby keeping us alert and more in sync with our wake cycle.

Although low-intensity lighting can slow the onset of sleep and drowsiness (Campbell & Dawson 1990), Aoki and colleagues (1998) suggest that students should not be exposed to long periods of dim light, such as in a darkened lecture hall. In a study involving two simulated eight-hour night shifts, Campbell and Dawson also found that young adults maintained significantly higher levels of alertness and wakefulness when exposed to bright ambient lighting (1,000 lux) rather than dim ambient lighting (10-20 lux). Typical room lighting is approximately 2,500 lux compared to typical outdoor lighting, which generally averages about 10,000 lux.

Students in brightly lit classrooms will perform better in school compared to students in dimly lit classrooms (London 1988). In addition, sustained exposure to bright light also reduces eye fatigue during close work activities, making it easier to read and solve complex problems. Beyond this, there's a consistent body of evidence that suggests sunlight enhances mood (Harmatz, et al. 2000; Michalon, et al. 1997) and when we feel better, we usually perform better.

Bright natural sunlight is best for learning. Fluorescent lights have been shown to increase cortisol levels, a change likely to suppress the immune system. The flickering quality and barely audible hum emitted by fluorescent lights have a very powerful impact on our central nervous system.

Many schools confronted with the need for cost-savings have introduced "low-light days" to save on electrical bills. This is a mistake. The Department of Education in Alberta Canada showed that students enrolled in schools with above-average lighting had higher attendance, higher physical growth rates (averaging 10 millimeters), increased concentration, and better academic performance. Schools electricity requirements are so great that the real cost-savings may be in building skylights and even solar panels. But the evidence comes down hard against "low-light" days for kids. Keep the classrooms bright and find other ways to cut costs.

Strategies You Can Use

- ☞ Maintain a constant, adequate level of bright lighting (at least 2,000 lux) in your classroom. Bright lighting helps reduce drowsiness in class by suppressing the production of melatonin in the brain.
- ☞ Limit student exposure to darkened lecture halls and similar environments for extended periods. When such exposure is necessary, include low-level background lighting (from a hallway or a window).
- ☞ During periods of limited sunlight in the fall and winter, encourage learners to get proper exercise. Take them on frequent field trips and brisk walks, and hold PE classes outdoors when possible, rather than in a gym. Incorporate ample movement in the classroom, as well.
- ☞ During periods of decreased sunshine in October through March, make sure students are exposed to as much natural sunlight as possible; open classroom blinds and skylights.
- ☞ If a student appears depressed during fall and winter months, encourage the parents to consult with their child's physician.
- ☞ Deviate from the norm and take students outside for occasional learning sessions. Not only will they be exposed to more sunlight and fresh air, their brains will be stimulated by the novelty of learning in a new and different environment.

Bottom Line

Many learners may be under-performing simply because of lighting. Low light makes close work difficult on the eyes and nervous system. It also induces sleep and drowsiness. Indirect, but bright natural lighting is best for learning. Therefore, keep blinds open to take advantage of the ambient sunlight. As with room temperature, teachers need to have control over the amount of lighting in their rooms.

Color and Cognition

Our visual system takes in approximately 100 million bits of information per second: This is more than any other of our five senses. Much of our brain, in fact, is devoted to processing what we see. Considering this, how much might the colors around us impact our brain and learning?

Scientists are beginning to understand what advertisers have long suspected: Color can enhance moods, emotions, and behaviors—and possibly cognition, as well. Why the brain responds more positively to one color over another is still not understood. However it is a process likely begun during infancy when exposure to color, especially bright colors, plays an important role in stimulating and strengthening immature neural connections in the brain's occipital lobe or primary visual cortex.

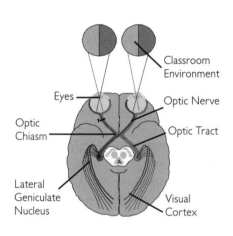

Exposure to color is also known to play a key role in the maturation and stimulation of brain areas outside the occipital lobe/visual cortex. These areas include the parietal lobe (touch and spatial understanding), the limbic system (emotional message encoding), the temporal lobes (hearing and language), and the frontal lobe (body movement, decision-making, attention, reasoning, and memory). As such, it is not surprising that studies suggest full color multi-media images produce significantly better recall than black-and-white visuals in complex learning situations (Farley & Grant 1976). College students taking midterm exams printed on blue paper outperformed students taking the identical exam on red paper (Sinclair, et al. 1998). The color blue has been found to produce a calming effect conducive to deep thinking and concentration, while red is useful for creative thinking and short-term high energy (Birren 1978).

Color can also enhance memory of text when the colors are used in close proximity to words and in groupings of shapes and forms (Wallace, et al. 1998). However, when color groupings were compared solely with figure-shape elements to test description recall among 286 college psychology students in a seven-trial experiment, figure-shaped elements elicited significantly more functional descriptions than did colors (Harris & Amundson 1998). This suggests that figures can also act as important mnemonic devices.

Our reaction to color is a complex combination of biology, physics, and psychology, reports Trussel and colleagues (1997). Light in itself has no color (a fact which Issac Newton appreciated three centuries ago), but is known to evoke color perception in the eyes, and ultimately the brain. Studies conducted by Zeki (1993) located color-creating cells in the brain, namely the visual area of the striate cortex. Other research has found that the degree of neural and sensory stimulation triggered by color wavelengths and color saturation is believed to be the key determinant of how the brain responds to color (Robson 1999).

A study conducted by Boyatziz and Varghese (1994) found that young children responded overwhelmingly better to bright colors such as red, pink, and blue over dark colors, such as brown, black, and gray. In addition, the study found that children's emotional reactions to bright colors became increasingly positive with age, and girls in particular showed a preference for brighter colors and a stronger dislike than boys of darker colors. Read and colleagues (1999) demonstrated that preschool children exposed to visually appealing wall colors, ceiling designs, and other physical environment changes exhibited more cooperative behavior after such exposure than before. Hephill (1996) notes that our preference for bright colors seems to continue into adulthood, with women responding more positively than men.

For instance, researchers Shaie and Heiss noted as early as 1964 that regardless of age or cultural background, short-wavelength colors—what we commonly call the warm colors (red, orange and yellow)—are highly arousing, although not necessarily pleasing. Conversely, longer wavelength hues—what we commonly call the cool colors (blues and greens)—have a calming, relaxing effect. The majority of people, the researchers noted, identify cool colors as the most pleasant.

Robson (1999) reported that people who were exposed to a red environment perceived their time spent there to be shorter than those exposed to a blue environment, even though the actual time was the same in both instances. This finding concurs with past studies, which found that short-wavelength colors, when compared to their cool counterparts, elicit a higher degree of stimulation and tension in subjects.

The color or texture of a finish material has also attracted attention. Finishes within reach of students should be cleanable, durable, and/or replaceable. Apart from the finish of materials, the perception of newness or cleanliness also affects learning. Equivalent schools were observed as one was repainted and the other was not. Brightly colored walls or high light levels increase glare and possibly unwanted heat gain through lamp radiation. Hard cleanable surfaces may simplify maintenance tasks but increase reverberation and reduce display-friendly wall spaces. For greater cognitive impact in your various living/working/learning environments, consider these color tips:

✔ Classroom and Office Spaces: Best color is sky-blue tinged with red. This combination is conducive to thoughtful study, but also to alertness.
✔ Cafeteria: Best color is purple, which is known in the restaurant industry as a tranquilizing color that is good for the appetite.
✔ Gym: Best colors are yellow, orange, and coral, which represent the energizing hues.
✔ Add color to reports, presentations, and visual displays for better recall.
✔ Use a color laser printer or inkjet for printed handouts in class and experiment with printing exams on blue paper.

Classroom walls can be used to support useful peripherals and visuals. Simple enhancements can be made with color. The shades, tones and hues you use on the walls are important. Color consultants suggest that the predominant colors ought to be a subtle green with yellow, orange, and blue used as highlight colors. Some teachers have found certain yellows to work well also. The colors around us influence our mind states and create unconscious reactions. Wood paneling or a brick-face can create a warm, home-like feeling.

Bottom Line

We may be vastly underutilizing the potential of color in the learning environment. Use color handouts and overhead transparencies. Consciously choose the colors you use in the classroom; hang colorful posters; and encourage the use of color in mindmapping activities.

The Power of Peripheral Stimuli

For maximum absorption of your most important instructional content, post visuals on side walls of the classroom above eye level. Do not purposely draw attention to the postings, but allow students to discover them for themselves. Since subconscious peripheral messages are often more powerful than the standard front-of-the-room approach, be sure that all of your postings are positive, focused, interesting, and accurate.

When students, for example, are ready to learn grammar, post wall displays that feature only the most important grammar rule or the grammar rule of the week. Post the display a week before you actually cover the content. In this way, students begin to subconsciously embed the content and build a foundation for the upcoming lesson. Teaching at the semiconscious level is especially important for complex content such as math, foreign languages, and grammar—tasks that are traditionally taught exclusively with a conscious memorization approach.

Be very aware of the content of the messages you post. Sometimes what you might think of as a benign communication may have unanticipated ramifications. For example, consider the experience of an excellent teacher who had a class of learning-disabled students. She hung a poster with a nature scene and the message "Things take time" believing this would instill patience in her students. What actually came across to a student, however, was "you learn slowly, so don't expect too much, too soon." In another classroom a poster stated, "School is something we sandwich between weekends." The message actually conveyed was that "school gets in the way and weekends are what living is really about"—not exactly helpful content. Posters, however, that inspire, challenge, or provide support add much to the classroom environment. Just be aware of inadvertent connotations. A "You Can Do It" poster is much more effective, for example, than a "Hang In There, Baby" poster.

Your classroom should convey a feeling of confidence, joy, and curiosity. While the front of room is best kept neat and simple, post your most important instructional visual stimuli ought to be posted at the sides of the room. How often do you see student's eyes wandering around the room? Likely very often! One study found that while recall of lecture material decreased, recall of peripherals in the room actually increased.

Since the power of peripheral displays lies in their ability to impact students on the subconscious level, it is best not to draw conscious attention to them. Posting affirmations is an excellent way to start. One strategy suggests posting 5 to 15 light-colored poster boards with simple easy-to-read reminders for your students. They are most powerful when written in the first person (e.g., "I'm a Winner") rather than (e.g., "You're a Winner"). Posting signs above the door is especially potent, but remember to change them often and refer only occasionally to them in passing. The best thing about affirmations is that they work whether your students are 4 or 40.

Sample Affirmations

- ☞ I am a bright and capable learner.
- ☞ If you have learned something new today, give me five!
- ☞ Learning is fun, easy, and creative.
- ☞ I do new things simply, easily, and playfully.
- ☞ I am the change I want to see.
- ☞ For things to change, I must change.
- ☞ I am a unique and precious human being.
- ☞ Every problem offers a gift.
- ☞ I am a resourceful learner with many choices.

The actual positioning of visuals on the wall can make a difference in how students are impacted. For example, stronger feelings are evoked when a poster is *below* students' eye level, while right at *eye level* stimulates learners to talk about the poster. If you want students to simply notice information, such as in the form of a review, put it *above* eye level which stimulates the visual mode for recall.

Appropriately placed peripherals can effectively serve as:

✔ ***A Communication Board:*** To post assignments, reminders, messages, lost-and-found items, resources, and other pertinent bits of information. Post items you want students to talk about at eye level.

✔ ***Inspiration without Preaching:*** To offer messages in a way that students can "hear" them or read them without feeling lectured at or singled out. (e.g., "For things to change, I must change.")

✔ ***A Feedback Mechanism:*** To chart the progress of teams or the class as a whole; to highlight model papers or projects. Other possibilities include putting up collective mindmaps of the week in review, group art projects, student presentations, or a large graph or thermometer measuring class progress. Posting at eye level accesses more feelings of pride.

✔ ***Content Summaries:*** Post summaries or reminders of past learning as well as current subjects and sneak previews of future topics. Graphic organizers provide a great way to communicate a lot of information in a compact, visually appealing way.

✔ *Positive Affirmations:* Post bright-colored posters featuring encouraging messages, poetry, or inspiring quotes. Use a variety of pronouns (e.g., I, you, we, us, our), so that each has its own "voice." The more diverse the examples, the more students you'll reach.

✔ *Symbolic Material:* Post photos, posters, or illustrations that carry a powerful message without relying on text.

Bottom Line

A purposeful plan should be created for positively influencing students in ways beyond the stand-and-deliver, conscious-level approach. Add influences like posters on the wall and bulletin-board items. Assess the factors that are influencing your learning space. What feeling to students get when they walk into your room? Do they respond positively? Do both children and adults feel comfortable in the space? How might you improve the physical climate? In what ways might the emotional climate of your room be enhanced? A passive approach to surroundings can actually detract from learning. Make an effort to enhance your visual environment with interesting collections, photos, objects, and bulletin-board items that stimulate curiosity and the love of learning.

Visual Clutter Can Inhibit Learning

Although visuals and peripherals are usually positive, here's a twist: too much clutter is bad. Studies suggest that a disorganized or cluttered learning environment can impair cognition. Such environments cause the eye to dwell on a scene for significantly longer periods in an effort to "make sense" of the chaos—a task that requires substantial cognitive energy and detracts from meaningful learning time (Vecera, et al. 2000).

"Visual clutter," of course, does not refer to well-placed and thoughtful peripherals, but to an excess of disorganized stuff or unkempt areas.

A disorderly environment, research suggests, conflicts with the brain's natural tendency (occurring in the visual cortex and frontal lobe) to perceive our surroundings as an organized whole—a process necessary to obtaining meaning validity. How the brain perceives objects in relation to one another subconsciously guides our behavior and reaction to our environment, Ward and Duncan (1996) found.

Strategies You Can Use

- Make sure your classroom is physically neat before each learning session. If necessary, assign students to pick up papers, straighten desks, and perform other housekeeping tasks before class is dismissed. An untidy classroom can lead to a cluttered learning mind.
- Take care that ample classroom space is allotted for the storage and use of computers, audio-visual machinery, paperwork, and other materials not in use.
- Use appropriate wall space to organize material on bulletin boards.
- At least one time per month, take an honest stock of your classroom; freshen displays and discard materials no longer in use.

3 *What Students Hear*

Noise and Classroom Acoustics

Our amazing brain typically processes up to 20,000 bits of auditory stimuli every second. This means that nearly every sound in the range of 20 to 15,000 cycles per second is fair game for processing. Getting kids to hear what we *want* them to hear in the classroom, therefore, can be a problem.

In poorly designed classrooms that fail to address and reduce ambient noise, echo effects, reverberation, and other acoustical problems, student attention, off-task behaviors, and discipline problems increase—issues that take a serious toll on learning (Berg, et al. 1996). When learners have to strain to hear what their teacher is saying and teachers have to constantly adjust their volume to compete with ambient noise, valuable content learning time is sacrificed, unconsciously if not consciously.

Lawrence Feth (1999), professor of Speech and Hearing Science at Ohio State University, conducted an extensive acoustical study of classrooms. He found that many classrooms are acoustically unsound, which makes listening and learning difficult for children. In fact, the study found that of the 32 classrooms studied (in Central Ohio primary schools), only two (6%!) met the acoustical standards recommended by the American Speech- Language-Hearing Association (ASHA). The majority of class-rooms in the study had enough background noise and echoes present to hamper the learning of children with even *mild* hearing problems.

Children for whom English is a second language and children with hear-ing or learning deficits, have an especially hard time following what a teacher says in a noisy classroom. Smaldino and Crandell (2000) note that hearing-impaired and at-risk children have difficulty separating the teacher's message from background noise. Therefore, these learners may require technology devices specifically designed to improve the class-room's signal-to-noise ratio. Moreover, recent research strongly suggests poor acoustical conditions negatively impact students with normal hearing, as well (Nelson & Soli 2000; Smaldino & Crandell 2000).

Even more than a decade ago, Pekkarinen and Wiljanen (1990) reported dramatic improvement in students' speech discrimination after classrooms were refitted with sound-absorbing material that reduced ambient noise.

Acoustical experts know that children are especially sensitive to overly noisy classrooms because they are still learning language and need to clearly hear new speech sounds for effective acquisition. Conversely, adults have a larger vocabulary, which helps them mentally compensate when they can't hear clearly. Beyond causing an immediate stress response in the nervous system and the voluntary muscular reflex system (including the release of such neurotransmitters as epinephrine, norepinephrine, and cortisol), loud noise also increases heart rate, grimacing, and sudden muscle flexion. Together, these stress responses impair learning over time.

Feth (1999) reported that the most prominent sources of background noise in classrooms (both new and old) are the heating and cooling systems. In addition, classrooms tend to have *hard* walls and floors—surfaces that facilitate reverberation and interfere with speech recognition and understanding. Acoustical liveliness is a product of room configuration (parallel walls), surface finishes (hard, soft), material density (solid, hollow) and air tightness (sound transfer). A room designed for music is constructed very differently than one designed for quiet conversation. Shower spaces, for example, are great for singing but poor for conducting discussions. If group activities are more prevalent than lectures, rooms should be more absorptive of sound. Learning is hampered when the teacher or students do not have a common language or when students are unfamiliar with a new concept and the teacher does not clearly enunciate.

Disturbing "echoes" or "flutters" can be mitigated by angling walls at least 5 degrees out of their original parallel plane, and by placing hard wall surfaces, (i.e., glass, marker boards, etc.) opposite a storage area, door, or other uneven feature versus a hard even surface. Carpeted floors and acoustical ceilings also reduce reverberation (sound that continues to bounce). Solid walls or ones with sound insulation prevent exterior noise transfer, but only if there is no air gap (walls only to the bottom of suspended ceilings do not help). When windows or doors are open, a low-frequency sound device (i.e., "white noise") can help mask ambient sounds.

Excessive environmental noise—including traffic sounds, aircraft noise, machinery, beepers, and even casual conversation—can reduce comprehension and work performance, especially in the early stages of learning a new task (Gomes, et al. 1999; Berglund, et al. 1996). The Environmental Protection Agency recommends that noise levels generally not exceed an average of 45 decibels in the daytime and 35 decibels at night. Unfortunately, ambient or environmental noise in many urban areas often reaches 70 decibels in the day and more than 60 decibels at night. In comparison, a whisper is approximately 20 decibels and a stereo at full blast is about 120 decibels.

Fortunately, an effort is being made by a broad-based coalition of engineers, audiologists, parents, educators, and architects to develop a national standard for school acoustics (Sorkin 2000). The standards would comply with codes promulgated by the Americans with Disabilities Act.

While scientists have known for some time that chronic noise can have a negative effect on academic performance, a recent study suggests that noise may actually *prevent* children from acquiring speech recognition skills (Evans & Maxwell 1997). Evans and Maxwell compared children in a noisy school (in the flight path of a New York international airport) with similar children in a quiet school. Unlike subjects in other noise studies, both groups of children were tested in quiet conditions. This method allowed the researchers to eliminate an important variable. By testing subjects in a quiet room, they demonstrated that decreased reading scores are due to *chronic* noise exposure—not noisy *episodes* that might have occurred during the testing sessions.

The study compared 116 first- and second-graders from two elementary schools. Children in one school regularly experienced peaks of up to 90 decibels of noise every 6.6 minutes by low-flying jet aircraft. The other school—closely matched with the first school in ethnicity and family income levels—was in the same urban area but in a quiet neighborhood.

Each child was given an auditory screening test and then assessed for abilities to read, distinguish words with background noise, distinguish sounds with background noise, and distinguish word sounds (phonemes) under quiet conditions. Results indicated children chronically exposed to aircraft noise had significant deficits in reading. The researchers believe that noise-induced reading problems may be partly due to deficits in language acquisition, since the chronically exposed children also suffered from impaired speech perception.

In an earlier study, Smith and Stansfield (1986) found a link between high exposure to aircraft noise and an elevated frequency of everyday errors among adults (i.e., forgetting appointments, dropping things, confusing right from left). In addition, an earlier study led by Evans (1995) identified deficits in reading, long-term memory, and speech perception among 135 third- and fourth-graders exposed to aircraft noise.

Noise may have physiological implications in addition to cognitive ones. For example, Evans and colleagues (2001) found that children in noisier areas had higher blood pressure, heart rates, and elevated stress levels—factors that aren't conducive to learning. Scientists know that excessive chronic stress causes the brain to release abnormal levels of cortisol, a hormone that finds receptors in the hippocampus, a brain area important to memory and learning. Over time (1-2 months), acute levels of cortisol can kill brain cells and inhibit recall.

Strategies You Can Use

- Take stock of the noise level in your classroom. Do you notice students straining to hear you or their fellow classmates? Do you have hearing-impaired students or those who speak English as a second language? These students, especially, may experience difficulty understanding speech in a noisy classroom.
- Consider softening the noise level in your classroom by hanging egg cartons or tapestries on the walls.

- If you suspect a significant problem with ambient noise, consult your school administration or an acoustical engineer on the most efficient way to eliminate the distractions. Allergy-sensitive carpeting, drapery, sound absorbing panels, wall hangings, and commercially available sound amplification systems may be options to explore.
- Make appropriate use of soothing "white noise" or music at suitable times to mask disturbing noise. Some options include fish tanks, desktop waterfalls, and classical/environmental music.
- It is especially important to maintain a quiet environment when learners are taking exams or when other important mental tasks are required. Schedule tasks that require the most intense mental concentration when environmental noise levels are the lowest.
- Do your part to see that school planners and administrators know the research that suggests children who attend schools near noisy airports, major roads, and railways may not learn to read as well as children in quiet schools.

The Learning Benefits of Music

There are various ways to derive the benefits of music in learning. Simply playing baroque in the background on low volume can evoke a relaxed and optimal learning state. Depending on the type of music played, you can also use it to help learners cool down, warm up, relax, or get energized. Beyond influencing mood, some educators use music to carry positive messages. Frequent music playing will increase the pleasure of learners and give them the feeling that their classroom is a happy, pleasant place to be.

Learner preference is an important consideration when incorporating music into your lesson plans. Like room temperature, preferences among learners vary. For some, low-level background music (such as baroque in a major key) will be ideal, while others will prefer nature sounds or popular tunes with inspirational lyrics. Variables include learner's cultural back ground, learning-style preferences, personality type, and prior exposure. Volume level, music type, and instruments featured are other important factors. The best results will be achieved by experimenting with your particular group of learners and by using music sparingly.

If you play music all the time, learners will habituate to it and it will stop being effective. Therefore, be sure to use music purposely and judiciously. Choose the type of music you play with care. Consider what target states you wish to achieve and take into account your student total demographics. Typically use music no more than 5 to 20% of your class period.

For example, to *calm* students down, choose a slow (40-50 beats per minute) song—slightly slower than the normal heartbeat, which is 60-70 beats per minute. You might try, for example, "Peace and Quiet" by Harry Pickens or nature sounds. To *motivate* students, on the other hand, choose a fast beat selection (120-140 beats per minute), such as "Transitions to Go," produced by The Brain Store® or a club remix or popular dance tunes. And to enhance productivity, choose selections that mirror the normal human heart rate (60-70 beats per minute) and are highly predictable and in a major key. You might try, for example, "smooth jazz" or "Whistle While You Work"—a popular Brain Store® CD.

Although some students require total quiet to concentrate, others learn best in a noisy, busy environment. In one study, for example, one-fifth (20%) of elementary-school-age learners preferred a noisy environment to a quiet one (Carbo, et al. 1986). The majority of learners, however, prefer a quiet environment during intense concentration, and even subtle extraneous noise can be an obstacle for these learners.

Researchers at the University of Evansville discovered, for example, that certain electronic devices (e.g., VDTs) produce a barely audible high-frequency tone that induces stress and impairs learning. Women in the study were especially impacted by the noise. The researchers reported an 8% loss of productivity in some subjects. The noise may be more detrimental to women due to their better hearing, the study concluded.

Bottom Line

The amount of stimulation that the human brain can receive and integrate is astonishing. What students *hear* in the classroom is just as important as what they *see* and *feel*. While your room may be visually attractive, 20-30% of your students learn best through sound. Hence, it is a good idea to include music and other auditory learning devices (i.e., story-telling, books-on-tape, nature sounds, etc.) in your lesson planning. Beyond affecting attitudes and evoking specific desirable mood changes, certain music has been shown to enhance learning and recall.

If possible, use a sound-system with the speakers positioned as high as possible in the room and secured to the walls or ceiling. The music player can be kept in a desk drawer or in a locked storage area when not in use. Good acoustical design will make hearing and paying attention easier for students.

It is a good idea to have a variety of music types available. When deciding which type to play, observe the state of your learners. If they are lethargic and you want to motivate them, put on faster-paced music, such as instrumentals or exciting movie themes at 120+ beats per minute. If they are hyperactive or restless, put on slower-paced music with 40 to 60 beats per minute. Some teachers play lively classical music at the start of class when students are arriving, slower music during moments of relaxation or test-taking, and upbeat music during activities. Your choice of music at the start of class sets the stage and tone for the entire session and, ideally, increases your students' and your own receptivity for learning.

4 *What Students Smell, Taste, and Breathe*

Aromas, Mood and Cognition

Like the rest of our senses, smell is a key component in learning and can, in some instances, improve cognition. But our ability to *detect* odor is especially important since it represents one of the most direct pathways to the brain (Dhong, et al. 1999). For example, Pauli and colleagues (1999) reported that undergraduate psychology students experienced significant cognitive enhancement in word-association and word-naming tests after being exposed to background odors of vanilla. Similar results were noted by Schnaubelt (1999) in learning environments using scents of lavender. And in a 40-minute test of vigilance (similar to that given to air traffic controllers and long-distance drivers), production workers that received 30-second bursts of peppermint or muguet (lily of the valley) every 5 minutes showed a 15 to 20% improvement in performance (Dember & Parasuraman 1993).

Research examining the effects of smell on cognition is ongoing, but preliminary evidence does point to a positive connection. According to Sullivan and colleagues (1998) patients with brain injuries performed equal to that of healthy control participants in a vigilance test after receiving periodic whiffs of peppermint. In addition, olfactory dysfunction is among the first signs of Alzheimer's disease and is often observed in other brain-related disorders such as schizophrenia (Moberg, et al. 1999; Vance 1999).

The effect of odor on sleep and relaxation has also been examined. Odors are thought to disrupt sleep and quicken the heart rate during slumber, except for one odor—heliotropine—a vanilla-almond fragrance.

One study, which used the scent on patients at the Memorial Sloan-Kettering Cancer Center in New York, netted encouraging results when the researchers found it relieved stress and anxiety among subjects (Kallan 1991).

Several aromas produce physiological arousal as measured by electroencephalogram recordings (Klemm et al. 1992) and self-reported emotional changes (Kikuchi et al. 1992; Nakano et al. 1992). The aroma of chamomile, for example, can put people in a better mood, according to Roberts and Williams (1992). Peppermint odor appears to be capable of causing very small electroencephalogram, electromyogram, and heart-rate changes during sleep (Badia, et al. 1990), and some odors can modify artificially induced sleep time in mice (Tsuchiya, et al. 1991).

Olfaction (the neuroscience of smell) influences our moods and levels of anxiety, fear, hunger, depression, and sexuality. Weiner and Brown (1993) report that Professor Baron at the Rensselaer Polytechnic Institute in Troy, New York found certain aromas inspire individuals to set higher goals for themselves, take on more challenges, and get along better with colleagues.

In experiments on neonatal rats, Sullivan and colleagues (1991) found that conditioned odor stimulation and tactile stimulation "are addictive in their effects on learning." The positive learning effects came from a peppermint odor injected into various norepinephrine receptor blockers, a procedure which allowed researchers to rule out other causes for the change.

Alan Hirsch (1993), a Chicago neurologist, found that certain floral odors increased subjects' ability to learn, create, and think. In an experiment that compared the puzzle ability (a thinking skill) of recovering patients against a control group, the researcher found that subjects exposed to a flowery scent solved the puzzle 30% faster than those who were not exposed to the scent.

While we are aware that being in a better mood can help cognitive performance, is there any direct evidence that aromas can enhance cognition? No; however, there is evidence that specific odors can better enable one to recall information learned in the presence of that odor (Smith, et al. 1992). This effect, however, may only be a case of context-dependent learning, so we need to be careful not to take the findings too far.

Context-dependent learning assumes that the context in which the original learning takes place provides cues that, when present, can enhance later recall. It's easier to remember your math, for instance, when you return to the classroom where you learned it. Thus, the stimuli itself (e.g., aroma, classroom, setting) does not produce the effect, but rather represents the original context. In other words, if the smell of peppermint wasn't present during the original state of learning, it won't help your recall later.

The olfactory regions are also rich receptors for endorphins, which generate feelings of pleasure and a sense of well being. The human brain's ability to detect changes in the environment is well documented. People can distinguish odors with tiny variations in the chemical structures of the odor molecule. Experiment with various aromas in your own classroom or office. Ask learners what they think. Do they feel energized and more alert after a whiff of peppermint? Do they feel relaxed and calm after a whiff of vanilla? How do they feel when surrounded with the aroma of chocolate chip cookies, a pumpkin-scented candle, or fresh baked bread? If nothing else, you'll enjoy watching your learners' eyes light up and their nostrils twitch when they walk into the room.

Strategies You Can Use

- Conduct your own class experiment using various scents. Do learners respond better to a light scent in the background, for example, or to a more intense or prominent scent? Do students seem to be more attentive after a whiff of peppermint or vanilla? Does either aroma seem to increase learners' sense of well-being? Record your results.
- Be sensitive to others' complaints about bothersome smells, such as perfume, food, or cigarette smoke. Unpleasant odors are known to inhibit learning. Also, be aware that some people are allergic to specific odors.

- Scents such as peppermint, lemon, jasmine, chamomile, and spiced apple are available in tea-bag form. Consider supplying them in as an alternative to soft drinks and coffee in staff lounges.
- In school offices or other waiting areas, consider keeping such scents as naturally fragrant wood furniture (cedar or cypress) or home-style fragrances such as potpourri in the room.

Bottom Line

Favorable Scents

Smell is an important sense that we have underutilized in the learning environment. An awareness of aromas, and what's been coined "aromatherapy," can provide a very powerful edge in reaching learners and influencing optimal learning states. Start simple.

Research suggests that peppermint, basil, lemon, cinnamon, and rosemary enhance mental alertness, while lavender, chamomile, orange, and rose calm nerves and encourage relaxation. However, a word of caution: Many of the commercially produced aromas are diluted with other chemicals that can cause an allergic response in some people. The simplest and purest aroma sold commercially is lavender, but real-food fragrances, such as fresh bread, cinnamon, peppermint, and lemon are a safer choice.

Toxic Air Pollutants Hinder Cognition

The air of many industrial cities is plagued by heavy metal pollutants such as cadmium and lead, in addition to toxic gases such as carbon monoxide. Research is revealing that these invisible toxins can have a detrimental effect on cognition in young learners. And because large urban areas are the most likely sites for industrial manufacturing plants, congested traffic, smog, and other sources of pollution, students living in these locations are often most affected (Halmiova & Potassova 1995).

In particular, overexposure to lead in early childhood is known to affect growth, memory, attention, reading skills, and learning in general, reports Yiin (2000). In addition, lead has been found to contribute to behavioral problems. How does this occur? Studies demonstrate that lead interferes with the  brain's transmission of a powerful and common neurotransmitter called dopamine, which is primarily involved in producing positive moods and coordinated body movements. Lead also inhibits activity in the hippocampus, a key memory-formation area of the brain. In a study examining 80 children (ages 8-9) living in an industrially polluted area, Halmiova (1995) found memory deficits in these children lasting over two years.

In a study of two separate groups of children and adults (ages 9-21), researchers found that participants living in highly polluted areas displayed lower cognitive performance in tasks requiring attention, memory, and reading compared to control subjects living in relatively clean areas (Potassova 1993). In an earlier study published in 1992, Potassova noted similar deficiencies in immediate and delayed recall among 83 children (ages 8-20) living in an industrially polluted area.

Researchers also found a probable link between Attention-Deficit/Hyperactivity Disorder and cadmium air pollution among 80 individuals (ages 2–29) residing in a polluted locale (Bateman 1992; Stewart-Pinkham 1989). Pollution, combined with urban noise and overcrowding, also causes stress and other physical symptoms, Ruback and colleagues (1997) found, while another study found a link between pollutants and asthma and respiratory infections (Sarafino & Dillon 1998).

Finally, the current ozone standard—established by the U.S. Environmental Protection Agency in 1990—states that an area must control pollutant emissions if the daily maximum ozone concentration exceeds 0.12 parts per million per hour on more than three occasions in a year. In spite of concerted efforts, many areas have yet to comply with this standard (Abelson 1997).

Impact of Negative Ionization

Have you ever heard of negative air? In spite of its label, this is a desirable thing. The air around us is electrically charged by many environmental factors, including cosmic rays, friction caused by air movement, radioactive dust, ultraviolet radiation, and atmospheric pressure changes. In areas of higher population, the atmosphere's healthy balance of positive to negative ions can be disrupted. Human activity, it seems, destroys negative ions and ultimately reduces the amount of oxygen in the air. Smoke, dust, smog, pollutants, electrical emissions, heating systems, coolers and traffic exhaust are all culprits. The air becomes too highly electrified (too many positive ions) and the human reaction is counterproductive to learning.

When it comes to air, the more negatively charged it is, the better. When the electrical charge in the air is too positive, it can cause you to feel groggy, lethargic, sleepy, or depressed. Have you ever noticed how when you stand in front of a waterfall, or step outdoors just after a rain, or stand atop a mountain, or just get out of a shower, you feel fresh and energized. You may be enjoying the benefits of negative ionization.

Just for the sake of comparison, a stuffy classroom may have an ionization count of say +1000, while that spot in front of the waterfall has an ionization level closer to -100,000. This difference can have a powerful effect on learning.

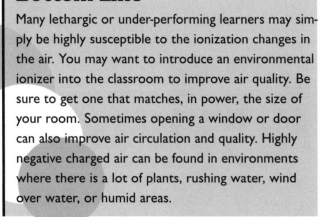

Bottom Line

Many lethargic or under-performing learners may simply be highly susceptible to the ionization changes in the air. You may want to introduce an environmental ionizer into the classroom to improve air quality. Be sure to get one that matches, in power, the size of your room. Sometimes opening a window or door can also improve air circulation and quality. Highly negative charged air can be found in environments where there is a lot of plants, rushing water, wind over water, or humid areas.

Spider Plant

Can Plants Improve Learning?

Scientists at the National Aeronautics and Space Administration have discovered that the use of plants creates a better scientific, learning, and thinking environment for astronauts (Wolverton, 1996). Could this research also apply to other indoor learning environments? Dr. B.C. Wolverton, who headed up NASA's Environmental Research Laboratory, says that certain plants improve life for the astronauts (and his own personal life at home) by removing pollutants from the air, increasing the negative ionization in the atmosphere, and charging the indoor air with oxygen. In fact, Federal Clean Air Council studies found that plants raised indoor oxygen levels and increased productivity by 10%. A single plant can increase productivity in 100 square feet of space.

Best Plants for Clean Air

✔ Palms
✔ Dracaena
✔ Rubber Plants
✔ English Ivy
✔ Ficus
✔ Boston Ferns
✔ Spider Plants

Dracaena

English Ivy

Have you ever taken a class or workshop in a sterile, stark classroom or conference room and felt totally unresponsive? Consider whether you may have perked up in an environment filled with plants. Plants not only make the air cleaner and richer, they enhance the aesthetic environment. Most of us use only 10 to 25% of our lung's capacity with each breath we take. This is bad because stale air starves the brain. For optimal learning, provide your learners with fresh, uncontaminated, highly oxygenated air. The ideal humidity level is between 60 and 80%. Encourage your students to breathe deeply, and don't forget to do so yourself, especially when you're feeling stressed or pressured.

Bottom Line

We don't always realize the impact of the air we breathe; the pollutants around us may go unnoticed. These factors are, however, important to creating an optimal brain-friendly environment for learners. Plants are a great way to provide a nice aesthetic touch. They also help filter the air of toxins and increase oxygenation. Include four to eight plants in your classroom if it's of typical size (approximately 900 square feet). According to Wolverton (1996), the best plants for optimal air cleansing and oxygenation are: gerbera daisies, yellow chrysanthemums, ficus benjamina, philodendrons, dracaena deremensis, peace lilies, and bamboo palms.

Dehydration and Learning

As a general rule, drinking fountains are easy to find in today's schools. Cost concerns, however, are reducing their numbers; water quality has made them less attractive, and some teachers reduce student access to them during class because of discipline issues. This makes bottled drinking water an attractive alternative.

Scientists have long known that dehydration can lower attention and impair mental performance. In one study, for example, subjects with a 2% reduction in body weight from dehydration experienced a 10% reduction in scores on word-recognition and arithmetic tests (Gopinathan, et al. 1988).

At the other extreme, a new study (Rogers, et al. 2000) suggests that drinking *too much* water can also impair mental performance on cognitively demanding tasks. The study examined the effects of hydration by testing the reaction time of volunteers undergoing an intensive visual task. The task involved pressing a specific button on a keyboard in response to prompts on a computer screen. Subjects performed the task before and after drinking either four or ten ounces of water.

Subjects that rated themselves as *thirsty* and then drank 4 ounces of water, performed 5% better on the test. When the same subjects drank 10 ounces of water, they performed 10% better on the test. However, subjects who were *not thirsty* and drank water performed *worse* on the test. Non-thirsty subjects who drank 4 and 10 ounces of water respectively scored 10% and 15% lower on the test.

Although fluid needs vary among individuals, the findings suggest that drinking fluids in excess of perceived thirst can impair mental performance. Fortunately, the study also indicates that healthy people, under normal conditions, can rely on their sense of thirst to accurately replace fluids when dehydrated.

Overall, the study found that the ingestion of *any* food or fluid (even water) produces a short-term cognitive depletion brought on by the diversion of resources for digestion and absorption. Specifically, overhydration (drinking water when not thirsty) decreases the concentration of blood components that have been shown to influence mental activity. These components include glucose, insulin, insulin-like growth factor, and electrolytes (sodium, potassium, chloride, calcium, magnesium, and phosphate). To address this issue, Rogers (ibid) is now performing experiments to test the effect of adding glucose and elec-

trolytes to drinks. The researcher hopes to determine if these substances have an impact on the mental activity of non-thirsty individuals.

Learning specialists recommend eight to ten glasses of water per day depending on the individual's body size, weather, and activity level. Nutritionists recommend pure water to ensure that it is free of contaminants. Water is better for the body than coffee, tea, soft drinks, or fruit juices, as it is free of diuretic or sugar agents that can throw your body's natural rhythm off. Many teachers have found that both behavior and performance improve when they encourage students to drink water as often as necessary.

Bottom Line

Students who are bored, listless, drowsy, and lacking concentration may, in fact, be dehydrated. Talk to your students about the consequences of dehydration and the value of water. Remind learners to drink water on their breaks and at recess. Allow them to bring water bottles into the classroom. If you teach sessions that last more than 45 minutes, it is especially important to see that students have access to water during class.

5 · *The Total Environment*

School Facilities and Cognition: Do They Matter?

Research indicates that well-planned and enriched learning environments stimulate learning and reduce discipline problems. When orchestrated with other sound teaching strategies, brain-friendly learning environments strengthen neural connections and aid long-term memory, planning, and motivation, note researchers Frank and Greenberg (1994).

One study (Ayers 1999) examined the relationship between high school facilities and student achievement. The researchers used the Design Appraisal Scale for High Schools (DASH-I) to measure the different design variables and determine a total quality score for each school in the study. Based upon the results of the analyses, school-design variables explained approximately 6% of the variance in English and Social Studies performance; 3% in Science performance, and 2% in both Mathematics and Writing performance (ibid).

Another researcher (Anderson 1999) studied the influence of 38 middle-school design elements on student achievement as measured by the eighth-grade Iowa Test of Basic Skills (ITBS). The Design Appraisal Scale for Middle Schools (DASM) was applied during site visits. The analysis revealed that 27 of the 38 DASM design factors positively correlated to the composite ITBS scores. The most influential design elements included: (1) Multifunctional in nature; (2) Sufficient play areas; (3) Functional activity pockets; (4) Enough green areas; (5) Exit doors to the outside; (6) Overall positive impression; (7) Administration centrally located; and (8) Overall school aesthetics.

Learning Suffers in Poor Environments

Conversely, schools with shattered windows, broken-down restrooms, leaky roofs, insufficient lighting, and overcrowding have a significant negative impact on cognition. Such conditions are frequently found in many of our nation's schools, and, unfortunately, far too many children, especially those in poor urban areas, are schooled in dilapidated, crowded facilities. According to a comprehensive study by Cash and colleagues (1997) covering 325 public schools in three school districts,

the adverse effect these conditions had on academic performance was significant.

Cash found a positive relationship between building conditions and academic performance, delinquent behavior, and absenteeism. Her findings also suggest that quality facilities, coupled with strong academic programs appear to be conditions essential to student learning. Similar findings were reported in less comprehensive studies by Hines (1996) and Edwards (1992).

Approximately one-third of all public schools in the United States are in need of extensive repair or outright replacement, according to a 1996 report by the General Accounting Office. The cost of bringing these schools up to par is estimated at 112 billion dollars (Cash, et al. 1997). Ultimately, the condition of a school building rests upon the financial ability of the school board to make the needed repairs. And in most cases, school districts must rely on taxpayers' ability or willingness to help meet capital expenses.

Here's what happens when an ailing school facility is given a face lift: Dr. Lorraine Maxwell of Cornell and the Northeast Region recently completed a case study that examined the relationship between student achievement and facility condition. When the Syracuse City School District in New York underwent several elementary-school renovations beginning in 1984, student scores were tracked by the Pupil Evaluation Program (PEP) test before, during, and after the renovations. Maxwell analyzed math and reading scores of both third- and sixth-grade students for an 11- to 12-year period. A statistically significant relationship between upgraded facility condition and higher math scores was found, suggesting that quality of facilities does matter.

Designing "SMART" Schools

School-facility design has garnered much attention these days. With an increased interest in student performance as well as safety, the old bricks and mortar,"cheapest is best" notion is dead and buried. "Innovative school design" no longer refers merely to creating facilities that have a splashy, interesting exterior. Today it means that schools are socially smart, cognitively supportive, emotionally safe, and environmentally friendly. One of the leaders in this movement is Dr. Jeffrey Lackney, Assistant Professor at University of Wisconsin at Madison. He's been an advocate for the research on 'smarter' school design and for building brain-friendly learning environments. "We know enough that it's finally time to act," says Lackney.

Who is paying attention to the findings on school design and learning? Are the decision makers getting it? "Yes, but it takes time. Many are focused on short-term goals rather than the bigger picture," says Scott Milder of Texas-based SHW Group—a highly innovative architectural and engineering firm that specializes in sustainable and brain-friendly learning environments. SHW Group is nationally recognized for outstanding contributions to the design profession and has been given the Merit Award, the Shirley Cooper Award, and named one of top-20 design firms nationwide. They design schools with the whole community in mind, including safety, cognition, curiosity, economics, mood, attendance, ecology, and social factors. What is it that innovative school design firms are paying attention to nowadays? Here are some highlights:

Daylighting - We're seeing more natural lighting and better use of skylights. New vertical solar monitors can scoop the natural light and provide 100% of daily classroom light. The sunlight is drawn into the light monitor and bounced off a series of baffles to provide soft, evenly distributed daylight throughout the facility.

Walls/Floors – Issues include reducing sound reverberation, convenient cleaning options, and "eye-friendly" appearance and functionality. Acoustical liveliness is a product of room configuration (parallel walls), surface finishes (hard, soft), material density (solid, hollow), and air tightness (sound transfer). Built-in sound systems and a overhead projector networked to a classroom computer are ideal. Hard walls such as glass or marker boards should not oppose each other but set opposite a non-flat wall. Improvements in flooring include the reduction of harsh linoleum floors and the addition of more carpet and carpet tiles.

Temperature/Humidity/Ventilation – Issues include providing flexibility and classroom control so that teachers can maintain the appropriate comfort levels. Heating and cooling mechanisms should be independent for each classroom, simple to operate, and controllable by the teacher in each classroom.

Classrooms – Traditional classrooms will give way to multipurpose "learning studios" or "zones"—places where children can engage in specialized task-specific activities together. "Learning Streets" and atrium entranceways and sitting areas will replace nondescript, narrow corridors. Wider hallways without lockers reduce bullying, running, and discipline problems. Shorter, more socially compatible "cubbyholes" will replace the standard maze of uniform lockers. An atrium lobby (supervised of course) allows students to de-stress and write, draw, or reflect in creative ways between classes and before and after school.

School Size – Smaller overall facilities create a psychologically and emotionally better environment for growth. They are both ecologically sound and easier to integrate with the community. It is now possible to build and operate small campuses for 300 to 700 students for the same cost per student as schools that accommodate 500 to 1400 students. The amount of space per student does matter. Research at the School Design Lab in Georgia suggests that elementary schools with less than 100 square feet per student have lower overall scores on the Iowa Test of Basic Skills. Students 14 years or older should spend a significant part of their time— perhaps even as much as two or three days a week (chaperoned or supervised)—outside of the classroom, involved in community service and school-to-work programs. Schools will capitalize on the community's many learning resources like libraries, parks, local industry, and museums. Schools will not be the only place formal learning takes place, ultimately reducing the need for larger, more impersonal school facilities.

Staff Areas – Teachers and other academic personnel need comfortable spaces where they can get away from the hustle and bustle, to think, relax, plan, and reflect. To keep teachers from going crazy, smart schools provide at least three places to congregate and get support: (1) a quiet reflective spot for power-naps; (2) a learning center, library, or staff media center; and (3) a de-stressing/exercise area with a treadmill and stretch mat. Most businesses have an employee lounge and many provide facilities that nurture good health and well-being. Teachers, despite having one of the most stressful and under-supported professions in our society are lucky if they have one staff lounge per school that is the size of a large closet.

Decentralized Buildings with Multi-Age Opportunities – In addition to learning *studios*, innovative school environments have fewer corridors and more open areas both in and out of the classroom where social interaction is encouraged. Nowhere in our society is such strict age grouping found as in our schools. There is ample evidence that multi-age class groupings are developmentally better for children. This means providing better access between buildings and classrooms—a profound structural variation from the norm. It has implications for decentralized solar heating, natural cooling, daylighting, space planning, aesthetics, resource sharing, community involvement, and accessibility.

Source: SHW Group, Inc. • McKinney ISD

Ecology – Many schools include ecology in their curriculum, but the school itself, is commonly an ecological disaster. The majority use huge amounts of electricity, fail to recycle, and allow students little opportunity to engage in meaningful eco-projects. Recycling projects, natural water storage, wind generation, composting, and organic gardens make sense for many schools. Why not role model ways to balance the energy crisis? This is an area of knowledge that will profoundly impact the work and lives of the next generation. Students can learn how to prepare, plant, grow, maintain, and create food sources from the soil. They can learn how to conserve and manage power wisely, how to improve the environment, and how to sustain the earth for future generations.

Options – A significant challenge is trying to create optimal learning environments for *all* students. Obviously the environment matters; the trouble is providing for a *variety* of learning styles, preferences, activity types, and levels of understanding. Smart schools give teachers some choice. If, for example, a group of students needs a private space to organize a skit, they might use an adjoining room that other grades have access to as well. The school might have a designated art room or science lab or music studio. Each classroom this way doesn't need to "have it all," but has access to specific activity-appropriate areas. If teachers are to be held responsible for the quality of student learning, we need to give them more flexibility and control over their work environment.

Project Spaces – These project-oriented areas will have high ceilings with ample power, gas, worktables, and specialized equipment—places where students can work on long-term projects like the building of a solar-powered car or the production of a school play. These rooms should be multi-functional so that one student might be building an architectural model, for example, next to another group of students painting a large mural.

Designing Activity Areas – Younger children have a natural instinct for safety at school. For learning and exploring, they prefer a "refuge-type" subspace with some top or side protection and ample visibility for look-

Source: SAB Group, Inc.

ing out (Legendre & Fontaine 1991). This allows them to focus on their activities rather than the surrounding environment and to play intently with a feeling of protection. But if it is too small or their visibility is impaired, children are less likely to use the space.

You can create a cozy, safe feeling without spending additional monies. "Cubby-holes" and low bookcases, for example, can double as room dividers. Create a few semi-circle areas large enough to accommodate two to five children. At the middle-school and high-school levels, a variety of insets, alcoves, and smaller lounge type spaces provide a sense of greater personal safety. These can be built into media centers, cafeterias, and open areas. Section the areas off, thus creating "mini-activity zones," which encourage more affiliation, sustained activity, and cooperative play (DeLong 1991).

A Showcase School

McKinney Independent School District in North Texas built one of the nation's first "high-performance" schools, Roy Lee Walker Elementary. Designed in 2000 by the innovative SHW Group of Texas, this school combines what's best for safety, aesthetics, function, and cognition.

Major components of a sustainable school include protecting the environment, channeling daylight into classrooms to minimize the use of artificial light, using recycled products and materials, and incorporating the school's design into the academic program.

The slightly higher initial cost is offset by lower maintenance costs over the long haul. In addition to the standard elementary school curriculum, students at this millennium-year model school have the unique opportunity to study ecology. They measure wind and solar energy, feed their frogs and take care of the school's water habitat, learn in classrooms illuminated predominantly by the sun, water their bean plants (which they keep in the school's greenhouse) with harvested rainwater, and check the weather at the campus weather station. "Sustainable design meets today's needs without compromising the resources available to future generations," says James McClure, consulting engineer on the project, adding "studies are showing that the various environmental benefits of sustainable design also benefit our children in the classroom" (McClure, et al. 2000).

"When the different components of a 'high-performance' school are combined under one roof, environmental sensitivity becomes second nature to students," says Gary Keep, a lead architect on the McKinney school project. "And," he adds, "it gives teachers a host of meaningful resources to illustrate lessons in math, reading, writing, and especially science." "The school design has not only enhanced the environment for learning, but it's also a part of it" says Scott Milder, an associate with SHW Group. There's no doubt, this is the future of better school environments for learning.

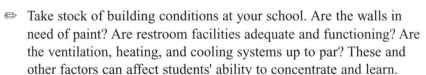
- Take stock of building conditions at your school. Are the walls in need of paint? Are restroom facilities adequate and functioning? Are the ventilation, heating, and cooling systems up to par? These and other factors can affect students' ability to concentrate and learn.
- Work with design and engineering firms that are well versed in the research on the effects of design and learning. Make sure your buildings are congruent with the environment as well.
- Work with your school administration and PTA to influence the condition of school facilities in positive ways. Ask PTA members to exert pressure on local officials to obtain funding from the city; organize volunteers to improve the environment; or support a political candidate or educational measure to bring about change.
- Form partnerships with area businesses to improve building conditions. For example, the Phoenix Union High School District formed a partnership with a private firm that offered the district financing and expertise in energy efficiency. The district received a substantial renovation grant that included future energy savings over a 10-year period—energy savings that will pay for the cost of renovation.

Bottom Line

Avoid being passive about the environment: It does matter. If new schools are being planned in your district, build alliances with key decision-makers and design firms that are well versed in the research on school design, learning, attendance, and cognition. Be proactive. Do what you can with what you have. If all you can modify is lighting, aroma, and seating, do that, at least. Sometimes business are willing to pitch in and provide materials, supplies, or financial support for school- or classroom-improvement projects. Remember that humans rarely perform at their best on their own. To learn, grow, behave, and perform optimally, a smartly designed, high-performance environment is necessary. Take charge; do your best to support your students in being their very best by orchestrating powerful learning environments.

Appendix

Resource List of Leading Educational Facility Planners

Cuningham Group—Minneapolis, Los Angeles, Madrid.
www.cuningham.com

DeJong & Associates—Dublin, Ohio. **www.djainc.com**

The EdDesigns Group—Ft. Lauderdale, Florida; Larry Rosen & Peter Gerber.
www.eddesigns.com

Edward Kirkbride, NCARB, REFP—Dowingtown, Pennsylvania; Architectural
Consultant for Urban Educational Facilities. **eek@bee.net**

Franklin Hill & Associates—Bellevue, Washington. **www.franklinhill.com**

Jeffrey Lackney, R.A., Ph.D., Department of Engineering, University of
Wisconsin-Madison; architect and consultant.
http://schoolstudio.engr.wisc.edu

KBD Planning Group—Bloomington, Indiana; Kathy Day.
www.kbdplanning.com

McKissick Associates PC—Harrisburg, Pennsylvania; Vern McKissick, AIA.
www.mckissickassociates.com

McKnight Associates—Ontario, Canada; Ronald McKnight.
rmck@allstream.net

SHW Architects and Planners—Dallas, Texas. **www.shwgroup.com**

Stanton Leggett & Associates—Larchmont, New York; Paul Abramson.
IntellEd@aol.com

Bibliography

Abelson, Philip. 1997. Proposed Air-Pollution Standards. *Science.* July 4. 277(5322): 15.

Andersen, Scott. 1999. The Relationship Between School Design Variables and Scores on the Iowa Test of Basic Skills. Doctoral Dissertation; The University of Georgia. 10/99.

Antoniadis, E.A.; C.H. Ko; M.R. Ralph; R.J. McDonald. 2000. Circadian rhythms, aging, and memory. *Behavioral Brain Research.* 111(1-2): 25-37.

Aoki, H.; N. Yamada; Y. Ozeki; H. Yamane; N. Kato. 1998. Minimum light intensity required to suppress nocturnal melatonin concentration in human saliva. *Neuroscience Letters.* Aug 14; 252(2): 91-4.

Aronen, E.T.; E.J. Paavonen; M. Fjallberg; M. Soininen; J. Torronen. 2000. Sleep and psychiatric symptoms in school-age children. *J. Am. Acad. Child Adolesc. Psychiatry.* 39(4): 502-8.

Asnis, J. 1999. Environmental factors in panic disorder. *Journal of Clinical Psychiatry.* Apr; 60(4): 264.

Ayers, Patti Dean. 1999. Exploring the Relationship Between High School Facilities and Achievement of High School Students in Georgia. Doctoral Dissertation; The University of Georgia. 12/99.

Badia, P., et al. 1990. Responsiveness to olfactory stimuli presented in sleep. *Physiology and Behavior.* 48: 87-90.

Bars, DR; F. Heyrend; CD Simpson; JC Munger. 2001. Use of visual evoked potential studies and EEG data to classify aggressive, explosive behavior of youths. *Psychiatric Services.* 52: 81-6.

Bateman, Barbara. 1992. Learning disabilities: The changing landscape. *Journal of Learning Disabilities.* 25(1).

Behling, Dorothy. 1994. School uniforms and personal perception. *Perceptual & Motor Skills.* 79(2): 723-9.

Behling, Dorothy; Elizabeth Williams. 1991. Influence of dress on perception of intelligence and expectations of scholastic achievement. *Clothing & Textiles Research Journal.* 9(4): 1-7.

Bellinger, David; Heather Foley Adams. 2001. Environmental pollutant exposures and children's cognitive ability. In *Environmental Effects on Cognitive Abilities.* Robert Sternberg and Elena Grigorenko (Eds). Mahwah, NJ: Lawrence Erlbaum Associates, Inc.

Bennett, S. Neville; David Blundell. 1983. Quantity and quality of work in rows and classroom groups. *Educational Psychology.* 32(2): 93-105.

Benton, D.; G. Roberts. 1988. Effect of vitamin and mineral supplementation on intelligence in a sample of school children. *Lancet.* Jan23; 1(8578): 140-3.

Berg, Frederick; James Blair; Peggy Benson. 1996. Classroom acoustics: The problem, impact, and solution. *Praxis der Kinderpsychologie und Kinderpsychiatrie.* Dec; 45(10): 16-20.

Berglund, B; P. Hassmen; R.F. Job. 1996. Sources and effects of low-frequency noise. *Journal of the Acoustic Society of America.* May; 99(5): 2985-3002.

Betts, Julian; Jamie Shkolnik. 1999. The behavioral effects of variations in class size: The case of math teachers. *Educational Evaluation & Policy Analysis.* Summer; 21(2): 193-213.

Birren, Faber. 1978. *Color and Human Response.* New York: Van Norstrand Reinhold.

Blader, J.C.; H.C. Koplewicz; H. Abikoff; C. Foley. 1997. Sleep problems of elementary school children: A community survey. *Archives of Pediatrics and Adolescent Medicine.* 151: 473-80.

Bosker, R.J. 1997. The end of class struggle? Background on the discussion of class size in primary education (Dutch). *Pedagogische Studieen.* 74(3): 210-27.

Boyatzis, C.J.; R. Varghese. 1994. Children's emotional associations with colors. *Journal of Genetic Psychology.* Mar; 155(1): 77-85.

Bradman, Asa; Brenda Eskenazi; Patrice Sutton, et al. 2001. Iron deficiency associated with higher blood lead in children living in contaminated environments. *Environmental Health Perspectives.* 109(10).

Brennen, Tim; Monica Martinussen; Bernt Ole Hansen; Odin Hjemdal. 1999. Arctic cognition: A study of cognitive performance in summer and winter at 69°N. *Applied Cognitive Psychology.* Dec; 13(6): 561-80.

Brenner, I.K.; J.W. Castellani; C. Gabaree; A.J. Young; J. Zamecnik; R.J. Shephard; P.N. Shek. 1999. Immune changes in humans during cold exposure: Effects of prior heating and exercise. *Journal of Applied Physiology.* Aug; 87(2): 699-710.

Burke, Stanley; Bob R. Stewart. 1980. The effects of temperature and protective clothing upon task completion time, work quality, and student attitude toward learning. *Journal of the American Assn. of Teacher Educators in Agriculture.* Nov. 21(13): 5-13.

Buxton, O.M.; M. L'Hermite-Baleriaux; U. Hirschfeld; E. Cauter. 1997. Acute and delayed effects of exercise on human melatonin secretion. *Journal of Biological Rhythms.* 12(6): 568-74.

Campbell, Scott S.; Drew Dawson. 1990. Enhancement of nighttime alertness and performance with bright ambient light. *Physiology & Behavior.* Aug; 48(2): 317-20.

Carlson, S; P. Rama; D. Artchakov; I. Linnankoski. 1997. Effects of music and white noise on working memory performance in monkeys. *Neuroreport.* Sept 8; 8(13): 2853-6.

Cash, Carol; Glen Earthman; Eric Hines. 1997. Building condition tied to successful learning. *School Planning and Management.* Jan; 21(1): 48-53.

Cheng, Yu-Ting; Andrew Van de Ven. 1996. Learning the innovation journey: Order out of chaos? *Organization Science.* 7(6): 593-614.

Cranz, Galen. 1998. *The Chair: Rethinking Culture, Body, and Design.* New York, NY: Norton.

Dahl, R.E.; N.D. Ryan; M.K. Matty; B. Birmaher; M. al-Shabbout; D.E. Williamson; D.J. Kupfer. 1996. Sleep onset abnormalities in depressed adolescents. *Biological Psychiatry.* 39(6): 400-10.

Dam, K.; F.J. Seidler; T.A. Slotkin. 2000. Chlorpyrifos exposure during critical neonatal period elicits gender-selective deficits in the development of coordination skills and locomotor activity. *Developmental Brain Research.* 121(2): 179-87.

DeBellis, M.D.; D.B. Clark; S.R. Beers, et al. 2000. Hippocampal volume in adolescent-onset alcohol use disorders. *American Journal of Psychiatry.* 157: 737-44.

Dember, W.; R. Parasuraman. 1993. Remarks before the American Association for the Advancement of Science. In: Pierce J. Howard, Ph.D. *Owner's Manual for the Brain.* 1994. Austin, TX: Leornian Press.

DeLong, A.J. 1991. Enhanced learning in child-care centers through design. In A.F. Torrice & R. Logrippo (Eds.) *Living and Learning Environments.* Design of the times: Day cafe. Burlingame, CA.

Dhong, H.J.; S.K. Chung; R.L. Doty. 1999. Estrogen protects against 3-methylindole-induced olfactory loss. *Brain Research.* Apr; 824(2): 312-5.

DeMitchell, Todd; Richard Fossey; Casey Cobb. 2000. Dress codes in the public schools: Principals, policies, and precepts. *Journal of Law & Education.* 29(1): 31-49.

Donovan, A.M; J.M. Halperin; J.H. Newcorn; V. Sharma. 1999. Thermal response to serotonergic challenge and aggression in attention deficit hyperactivity disorder. *Journal of Child Adolescent Psychopharmacology.* 9(2): 85-91.

Edwards, Maureen. 1992. *Building Conditions, Parental Involvement and Student Achievement in the D.C. Public School System.* Washington, D.C.: Georgetown University.

Ehrlichman, H.; S. Brown; J. Zhu; S. Warrenburg. 1995. Startle reflex modulation during exposure to pleasant and unpleasant odors. *Psychophysiology.* 32: 150-4.

Evans, Gary; Lorraine Maxwell. 1997. Chronic noise exposure and reading deficits: The mediating effects of language acquisition. *Environment & Behavior.* 29(5): 638-56.

Evans, G.; P. Lercher; M. Meis, et al. 2001. Community noise exposure and stress in children. *Journal of Acoustical Society of America.* 109(3): 1023-7.

Evans, G.; S. Hygge; M. Bullinger. 1995. Chronic noise and psychological stress. *Psychological Science.* 6(6): 333-8.

Farley, Frank; A.P. Grant. 1976. Arousal and cognition: Memory for color vs. black and white multimedia presentation. *Journal of Psychology.* Sep; 94(1): 147-50.

Feth, Lawrence. 1999. "Many Classrooms Have Bad Acoustics that Inhibit Learning." News release published by Ohio State University: December 21.

Finn, Jeremy; Charles Achilles; Helen Bain; John Folger. 1990. Three years in a small class. *Teaching & Teacher Education.* 6(2): 127-36.

Frank, D.A.; M.E. Greenberg. 1994. CREB: A mediator of long-term memory from mollusks to mammals. *Cell.* 79: 5-8.

Frasca-Beaulieu, K. 1999. Interior design for ambulatory care facilities: How to reduce stress and anxiety in patients and families. *Journal of Ambulatory Care Management.* Jan; 22(1): 67-73.

French, Nancy. 1993. Elementary teacher stress and class size. *Journal of Research & Development in Education.* Winter; 26(2): 66-73.

Garbarino, J. 1999. *Lost Boys: Why Our Sons Turn Violent and How We Can Save Them.* New York, NY: Free Press.

Gerrish, Carolyn, et al. 1998. Acute, early thermal experiences alter weaning onset in rats. *Physiology & Behavior.* June; 64(4): 463-74.

Gomes, L; P. Martinho; A. Pimenta; N. Castelo Branco. 1999. Effects of occupational exposure to low-frequency noise on cognition. *Aviation, Space & Environmental Medicine.* 70(3, Suppl): A115-18.

Gopinathan, P.M.; G. Pichan; V.M. Sharma. 1988. Role of dehydration in heat stress-induced variations in mental performance. *Archives of Environmental Health.* 43(1): 15-17.

Green, Kerry; Patricia Kuhl; Andrew Melzoff, et al. 1991. Integrating speech formation across talkers, gender, and sensory modality: Female faces and male voices in the McGurk effect. *Perception & Psychophysics.* 50(6): 524-36.

Grumet, Gerald. 1993. Pandemonium in the modern hospital. New England *Journal of Medicine.* Feb 11; 6(328).

Ha, Louisa. 1996. Advertising clutter in consumer magazines: Dimensions and effects. *Journal of Advertising Research.* 36: 76-84.

Halmiova, Olga. 1995. The effect of industrially polluted environment on memory performance in children. *Studia Psychologica.* 37(1): 3-10.

Halmiova, Ol'ga; Alena Potassova. 1995. Quality of life and the environment as a source of load for cognitive development in children. *Studia Psychologica*. 37(3): 206-8.

Hamers, J.H.; K. Sijtsma, et al. (Eds), 1993. *Learning Potential Assessment: Theoretical, Methodological and Practical Issues*. Amsterdam, Netherlands: Swets & Zeitlinger.

Harmatz, M.G.; A.D. Well; C.E. Overtree; K.Y. Kawamura; M. Rosal; I.S. Ockene. 2000. Seasonal variation of depression and other moods: A longitudinal approach. *Journal of Biological Rhythms*. 15(4): 344-50.

Harmon, D.B. 1951. The Coordinated Classroom. Research Paper: The American Seating Company, Grand Rapids, MI.

Harner, David P. 1974. Effects of thermal environment on learning. *CEFP Journal*. Mar-Apr; 12(2): 4-6.

Harris, L.J.; J.C. Amundson. 1998. Human classical conditioning of visual compound stimuli in paired-associate tasks. *Perceptual & Motor Skills*. Aug; 87(1): 227-41.

Hastings, Nigel. 2000. Children learn better when they sit in lines. Judith O'Reilly (Education correspondent) *Sunday Times* (London). www.Sundaytimes.co.uk/news/pages/sti/2000/1008/stinwenws01005.html.

Hastings, Nigel. 1995. Seats of learning? *Support for Learning*. (England) 10(1): 8-11.

Hemphill, M. 1996. A note on adults' color-emotion associations. *Journal of Genetic Psychology*. Sept; 157(3): 275-80.

Henning, Robert; P. Jacques; G. Kissel; A. Sullivan. 1997. Frequent short breaks from computer work: Effects on productivity and well being at two field sites. *Ergonomics*. Jan; 40(1): 78-91.

Heschong, Lisa. 1999. Daylighting in Schools: An Investigation into the Relationship Between Daylighting and Human Performance. A study performed on behalf of the California Board for Energy Efficiency for the Third Party Program administered by Pacific Gas & Electric, as part of the PG & E contract 460-000. For a copy, email Lisa Heschong at: info@h-m-g.com

Hines, Eric. 1996. *Building Condition and Student Achievement*. Blacksburg, VA: Virginia Polytechnic Institute and State University.

Hladky, A. and B. Prochazka. 1998. Using a screen filter positively influences the physical well being of VDU operators. *Central European Journal of Public Health*. Aug; 6(3): 249-53.

Hoffman, Allan. 1996. *Schools, Violence, and Society*. Westport, CT: Praeger Publishers/Greenwood Publishing Group, Inc.

Howard, Pierce, J. 1994. *The Owner's Manual for the Brain: Everyday Applications from Mind-Brain Research*. Austin, TX: Leornian Press.

Izard, C.E.; J Kagan; R.B. Zajonc (Eds). 1984. *Emotions, Cognition, and Behavior*. Cambridge, England: Cambridge University Press.

Jaschinski, W.; H. Heuer; H. Kylian. 1998. Preferred position of visual displays relating to the eye: A field study of visual strain and individual differences. *Ergonomics*. July; 41(7): 1034-49.

Joseph, Nathan. 1986.Uniforms and non-uniforms: Communication through clothing. *Contributions in Sociology*. Westport, CT: Greenwood Press.

Kallan, C. 1991. Probing the power of common scents. *Prevention*. Oct; 43(10): 39-43.

Kiger, Derrick. 1989. Effects of music information load on a reading comprehension task. *Perceptual & Motor Skills*. Oct; 69(2): 531-4.

Kikuchi, A., et al. 1992. Effects of odors on cardiac response patterns and subjective states in a reaction time task. *Psychologica Folia*. 51: 74-82.

Kim, Yunhee. 1999. Perceptions Toward Wearing School Uniforms. Dissertation Abstracts International. Feb. 59(8-A): 2917.

Klemm, W.R., et al. 1992. Topographical EEG maps of human response to odors. *Chemical Senses*. 17: 347-61.

Lackney, Jeffrey. 1994. "Educational Facilities: The Impact and Role of the Physical Environment of the School on Teaching, Learning and Educational Outcomes." Multi-disciplinary model for assessing impact of infrastructure on education and student achievement using applied research. Center for Architecture and Urban Planning Research, University of Wisconsin-Milwaukee.

Lanius, R.A.; P.C. Williamson; M. Densmore, et al. 2001. Neural correlates of traumatic memories in Posttraumatic stress disorder: A functional MRI investigation. *American Journal of Psychiatry*. 158: 1920-2.

Laurent, G. 1997. Olfactory processing: Maps, times, and codes. *Current Opinion in Neurobiology*. Aug; 7(4): 547-53.

Lazarus, S.M. 1996. The use of yoked base-up and base-in prism for reducing eyestrain at the computer. *Journal of American Optometric Association*. Apr; 67(4): 204-8.

Legendre, A.; A.M. Fontaine. 1991. The effects of visual boundaries in two year-olds' playrooms. *Children's Environment Quarterly*. 8: 1-16.

Liberman, J. 1991. *Light: Medicine of the Future*. Santa Fe, NM: Bear & Company Publishing.

Linton, Steven; Anna-Lisa Hellsing; T. Halme; K. Akerstedt. 1994. The effects of ergonomically designed school furniture on pupils' attitudes, symptoms, and behavior. *Applied Ergonomics*. Oct; 25(5): 299-304.

London, Wayne. 1988. Brain/Mind Bulletin Collections. *New Sense Bulletin*. (Los Angeles, CA) April; Vol. 13: 7c.

MacLaughlin, J.A.; R.R. Anderson; M.F. Holic. 1982. Spectral character of sunlight modulates photosynthesis of previtamin D3 and its photo-isomers in human skin. *Science*. May; 216(4549): 1001-3.

Mandai, O.; A. Guerrien; P. Sockeel; K. Dujardin; P. Leconte. 1989. REM sleep modifications following a Morse code learning session in humans. *Physiological Behavior*. 46(4): 639-42.

Maquet, P. 2000. Experience-dependent changes in cerebral activation during human REM sleep. *Nature Neuroscience*. 3(8): 831-6

Mark, Leonard S.; Marvin Dainoff; R. Moritz; D. Vogele. 1991. *Cognition and the Symbolic Processes: Applied and Ecological Perspectives*. Hilldale, NJ: Lawrence Erlbaum Associates.

Marx, Alexandria; Urs Fuhrer; Terry Hartig. 1999. Effects of classroom seating arrangements on children's question asking. *Learning Environments Research*. 2(3): 249-63.

McClure, James; James Estes; Gary Keep. 2000. "Sustainable Features of McKinney ISD Elementary School." Paper presented at the 12th Sympposium on Improving Building Systems. May 16; Sponsored by Texas A & M University, Texas State Energy Conservation Office, & The Department of Energy.

Michalon, Max; Gail Eskes; Charles Mate-Kole. 1997. Effects of light therapy on neuropsychological function and mood in seasonal affective disorder. *Journal of Psychiatry & Neuroscience*. Jan; 22(1): 19-28.

Miller, Ann; William Obermeyer; Mary Behan; Ruth Benca. 1998. The superior colliculus-pretectum mediates the direct effects of light on sleep. *Proceedings of the National Academy of Sciences*. July; 95: 8957-62.

Moberg, P.; R. Agrin; R. Gur; C. Reuben; B. Turetsky; R. Doty. 1999. Olfactory dys function in schizophrenia: A qualitative and quantitative review. *Neuropsychopharmacology.* Sept; 21(3): 325-40.

Moore, M.M.; D. Nguyen; S.P. Nolan; S.P. Robinson. 1998. Intervention to reduce decibel levels on patient care units. *American Surgeon.* Sept; 64(9): 894-9.

Mosteller, Frederick. 1995. The Tennessee study of class size in the early school grades. *Future of Children.* Summer-Fall: 5(2): 113-27.

Mrosovsky, N. 1999. Further experiments on the relationship between the period of circadian rhythms and locomotor activity levels in hamsters. *Physiological Behavior.* 66(5): 797-801.

Murphy, Mary Louise. 1998. Public School Uniforms: A Case Study of One School's Experience. Dissertation Abstracts International. June. 58(12-A): 4561.

Nakano, Y., et al. 1992. A study of fragrance impressions, evaluation, and categorization. *Psychologica Folia.* 51: 83-90.

Nelson, Peggy; Sig Soli. 2000. Acoustical barriers to learning: Children at risk in every classroom. *Language, Speech & Hearing Services in Schools.* 4: 356-61.

Nettles, Sandra; Wilfridah Mucherah; Dana Jones. 2000. Understanding resiliences: The role of social resources. *Journal of Education for Students Placed at Risk.* 5(1,2): 47-60.

Nishioka, Marcia; Hazel Burkholder; Marielle Brinkman, et al. 1996. Measuring transport of lawn-applied herbicide acids from turf to home: Correlation of dislodgeable 2,4 D turf residues with carpet dust and carpet surface residues. *Environmental Science & Technology.* 30(11): 3313-20.

Pauli, P.; L.E. Bourne; H. Diekmann; N. Birbaumer. 1999. Cross-modality priming between odors and odor-congruent words. *American Journal of Psychology.* 112(2): 175.

Pekkarinen, Eeva; V. Wiljanen. 1990. Effect of sound-absorbing treatment on speech discrimination in rooms. *Audiology.* Jul-Aug; 29(4): 219-27.

Pellegrini, Anthony; D.F. Bjorklund. 1997. The role of recess in children's cognitive performance. *Educational Psychologist.* Winter; 32(1): 35-40.

Potassova, Alena. 1993. Environmental neurotoxins and the level of attention and memory performance of children. *Studia Psychologica.* 35(1): 23-32.

Potassova, Alena. 1992. Serial position effect: Indicator of environmental-toxic injury? *Studia Psychologica.* 34(2).

Read, Marilyn; A. Sugawara; J. Brandt. 1999. Impact of space and color in the physical environment on preschool children's cooperative behavior. *Environment and Behavior.* May 31(3): 413-4.

Reed, H.L.; K.R. Reedy; L.A. Palinkas, et al. 2001. Impairment in Cognitive and Exercise Performance during Prolonged Antarctic Residence: Effect of Thyroxine Supplementation in the Polar Triiodothyronine Syndrome. *The Journal of Clinical Endocrinology and Metabolism.* 86: 110-16.

Roberts, A.; J. Williams. 1992. The effect of olfactory stimulation on fluency, vividness of imagery and associated mood: A preliminary study. *British Journal of Medical Psychology.* 65: 197-9.

Robson, Stephani. 1999. Turning the tables: The psychology of design for high-volume restaurants. *Cornell University Hotel & Restaurant Administration Quarterly.* June; 40(3): 56-65.

Rogers, P.J.; A. Kainth; H.J. Smit. 2000. A drink of water can improve or impair mental performance depending on small differences in thirst. *Appetite.* 36: 57-8.

Rona, R.J.; M.C. Gulliford; S. Chinn. 1998. Disturbed sleep: Effects of sociocultural factors and illness. *Archives of Disease in Childhood.* 78: 20-5.

Rosenthal, Norman. 1998. *Winter Blues: Seasonal Affective Disorder.* New York, NY: The Guilford Press.

Ruback, R. Barry; Janek Pandey; H.A. Begum. 1997. Urban stressors in South Asia: Impact on male and female pedestrians in Delhi and Dhaka. *Journal of Cross-Cultural Psychology.* 28 (1).

Sadeh, A.; A. Raviv; R. Gruber. 2000. Sleep patterns and sleep disruptions in school-age children. *Developmental Psychology.* 36(3): 291-301.

Salib, Emad. 1997. Elderly suicide and weather conditions: Is there a link? *International Journal of Geriatric Psychiatry.* Sept; 12(9): 937-41.

Sarafino, Edward; Joseph Dillon. 1998. Relationships among respiratory infections, triggers of attacks, and asthma severity in children. *Journal of Asthma.* 35(6).

Sateia M.J.; K. Doghramji; P.J. Hauri; C.M. Morin. 2000. Evaluation of chronic insomnia: An American Academy of sleep medicine review. *Sleep.* 23(2): 243-308.

Schnaubelt, K. 1999. *Medical Aromatherapy: Healing with Essential Oils.* Berkeley, CA: Frog.

Schroer, Sigrid. 2000. Self-organization—Order out of chaos: A little chaos is healthy. *Analytische Psychologie.* 31(2): 131-53.

Schwartz, Paul; Norman Rosenthal; Thomas Wehr. 1998. Serotonin 1A receptors, melatonin, and the proportional control thermostat in patients with winter depression. *Archives of Psychiatry.* Oct; 55(10): 897-903.

Sciutto, Mark J. 1995. Student-centered methods for decreasing anxiety and increasing interest level in undergraduate statistics courses. *Journal of Instructional Psychology.* 22(3): 277-80.

Shaie, K.W.; R. Heiss. 1964. *Color and Personality.* Bern, Switzerland: Hans Huber.

Sher, Leo; David Goldman; Norio Ozaki; Norman Rosenthal. 1999. The role of genetic factors in the etiology of seasonal affective disorder and seasonality. *Journal of Affective Disorders.* 53(3): 203-10.

Sher, Leo; Norman Rosenthal; Thomas Wehr. 1999. Free thyroxine and thyroid-stimulating hormone levels in patients with seasonal affective disorder and matched controls. *Journal of Affective Disorders.* 56(2-3): 195-9.

Silva, RR; M Alpert; D.M. Munoz; S. Singh; F. Matzner; S. Dummit. 2000. Stress and vulnerability to posttraumatic stress disorder in children and adolescents. *American Journal of Psychiatry.* 157: 1229-35.

Sinclair, Robert; A.S. Soldat; Melvin Mark. 1998. Affective cues and processing strategy: Color-coded examination forms influence performance. *Teaching of Psychology.* 25(2): 130-2.

Sinha, S.P., et al. 1998. Intelligence and vigilance performance as related to lead exposure among children. *Indian Journal of Clinical Psychology.* 25(2): 194-9.

Skrinar, G.S.; B.A. Bullen; S.M. Reppert; S.E. Peachey; B.A. Turnbull; J.W. McArthur. 1989. Melatonin response to exercise training in women. *Journal of Pineal Research.* 7(2): 185-94.

Smaldino, Joseph; Carl Crandell. 2000. Classroom amplification technology: Theory and practice. *Language, Speech & Hearing Services in Schools.* 4: 371-5.

Smith, Andrew; Stephen Stansfield. 1986. Aircraft noise exposure, noise sensitivity, and everyday errors. *Environment & Behavior.* 18(2): 214-26.

Smith, D.G., et al. 1992. Verbal memory elicited by ambient odor. *Perceptual and Motor Skills.* 74: 339-43.

Smith, Dwayne; Stephen Feiler. 1995. Absolute and relative involvement in homicide offending: Contemporary youth and the baby boom cohorts. *Violence & Victims*. Winter; 10(4): 327-33.

Sommers, Mary Kay. 1990. Effect of class size on student achievement and teacher behavior in third grade. Dissertation Abstracts International-A; 51/06 (Education, Curriculum and Instruction).

Sorkin, Donna. 2000. The classroom acoustical environment and the Americans with Disabilities Act. *Speech & Hearing Services in Schools*. 4: 385-8.

St. Otmer, V.E.; F.K. Mohammad. 1987. Ontogeny of swimming behavior and brain catecholamine turnover in rats prenatally exposed to a mixture of 2,4-dichlorophenoxyacetic and 2,4,5-trichlorophenoxyacetic acids. *Neuropharmacology*. 26(9): 1351-8.

Starr, Jennifer. 2000. School violence and its effect on the constitutionality of public school uniform policies. *Journal of Law and Education*. 29(1): 113-8.

Stevens, Joseph; Kenneth Choo. 1998. Temperature sensitivity of the body surface over the life span. *Somatosensory & Motor Research*. 15(1): 13-28.

Stewart-Pinkham, Sandra. 1989. Attention-deficit disorder: A toxic response to ambient cadmium air pollution. *International Journal of Biosocial & Medical Research*. 11(2): 134-43.

Sullivan, T.E.; B.K. Schefft; J.S. Warm; W.N. Dember; M.W. O'dell; S.J. Peterson. 1998. Effects of olfactory stimulation on the vigilance performance of individuals with brain injury. *Journal of Clinical and Experimental Neuropsychology*. Apr; 20(2): 227-36.

Taylor, H.L.; J. Orlansky. 1993. The effects of wearing protective chemical warfare combat clothing on human performance. *Aviation Space and Environmental Medicine*. 64(2): A1-41.

Terman, J.S.; M. Terman; E.E. Lo; T.B. Cooper. 2001. Circadian time of morning light administration and therapeutic response in winter depression. *Archives of General Psychiatry*. 58: 69-75.

Thodi-Petrou, C. 1998. Lead exposure and auditory processing: Behavior and physiological measures. Dissertation Abstracts International: Section B: the Sciences & Engineering; 59(5-B).

Tolan, P. 1996. How resilient is the concept of resilience? *Community Psychologist*. 4: 12-5.

Trinder, J.; S.M. Armstrong; C. O'Brien; D. Luke; M. Martin. 1996. Inhibition of melatonin secretion onset by low levels of illumination. *Sleep Research*. June; 5(2): 77-82.

Trussell, H. Joel; Jan Allebach; M. Fairchild; B. Funt; Wong P. Wah. 1997. Digital color imaging. *IEEE Transactions on Image Processing*. July 6(7): 897-9.

Tsuchiya, T., et al. 1991. Effects of olfactory stimulation on the sleep time induced by pentobarbital administration in mice. *Brain Research Bulletin*. 26: 397-401.

Umemura, M; K. Honda; Y. Kikuchi. 1992. Influence of noise on heart rate and quantity in mental work. *Annals of Physiology and Anthropology*. Sept; 11(5): 523-32.

Valent, F.; S. Brusaferro; F. Barbone. 2001. A case-crossover study of sleep and child-hood injury. *Pediatrics*. 2001. 107(2): E23.

Van Someren, E.J.; C. Lijzenga; M. Mirmiran; D.F. Swaab. 1997. Long-term fitness training improves the circadian rest-activity rhythm in healthy elderly males. *Journal of Biological Rhythms*. 12(2): 146-56.

van Toller, S. 1988. Odors and the brain. In *Perfumery: The Psychology and Biology of Fragrance*. S. van Toller and G. Dodd (Eds), London: Chapman & Hall. p. 121-46.

Vance, D. 1999. Considering olfactory stimulation for adults with age-related dementia. *Perceptual & Motor Skills*. Apr; 88(2): 398-400.

Vecera, S.P.; M. Behrman; J. McGoldrick. 2000. Selective attention to the parts of an object. *Psychoneurology Bulletin Review*. Jun; 7(2): 301-8.

Ververs, Patricia and Christopher Wickens. 1998. Head-up display: Effects of clutter, display intensity, and display location on pilot performance. *International Journal of Aviation Psychology*. 8(4): 377-403.

Wallace, David S.; S.W. West; A. Ware; D.F. Dansereau. 1998. The effect of knowledge maps that incorporate gestalt principles on learning. *Journal of Experimental Education*. Fall; 67(1): 5-16.

Wanzer, Melissa Bekelja; Ann Bainbridge Frymier. 1999. The relationship between student perceptions of instructor humor and student's reports of learning. *Communication Education*. 48(1): 48-62.

Ward, Robert; John Duncan. 1996. The slow time-course of visual attention. *Cognitive Psychology*. 30: 79-109.

Weetman, David; David Atkinson; James C. Chubb. 1998. Effects of temperature on anti-predator behavior in the guppy. *Animal Behaviour*. May; 55(5): 1361-72.

Weicker, H.; H.K. Struder. 2001. Influence of exercise on serotonergic neuromodulation in the brain. *Amino Acids*. 20(1): 35-47.

Weiner, Edith; Arnold Brown. 1993. *Office Biology*. Master Media Books, New York, NY.

Wheldall, Kevin; Yin Yuk Lam. 1987. Rows versus tables: The effects of two classroom seating arrangements on classroom disruption rate, on-task behaviour, and teacher behaviour in three special school classes. *Educational Psychology*. 7(4): 303-12.

Williamson, A.M.; A.M. Feyer. 2000. Moderate sleep deprivation produces impairments in cognitive and motor performance equivalent to legally prescribed levels of alcohol intoxication. *Occup. Environ. Med*. 57(10): 649-55.

Wolfson, A.; M. Carskadon. 1998. Sleep schedules and daytime functioning in adolescents. *Child Development*. 69: 875-87.

Yamada, N.; M. Martin-Iverson; K. Daimon; T. Tsujimoto; S. Takahashi. 1995. Clinical and chronobiological effects of light therapy on nonseasonal affective disorders. *Biological Psychiatry*. June 15; 37(12): 866-73.

Yiin, Lih-Ming. 2000. Childhood lead exposure peaks in warm months. *Environmental Perspectives*. Feb; 108(2).

Zeki, Semir. 1993. *Vision and the Brain*. Oxford, England: Blackwell Scientific.

About the Author

A former teacher and current member of the International Society for Neuroscience, **Eric Jensen,** has taught at all education levels, from elementary through university. In 1981, Jensen co-founded SuperCamp, the nation's first and largest brain-compatible learning program for teens, which now claims more than 25,000 graduates. He is currently President of Jensen Learning Corporation, in San Diego, California. His other books include *Music with the Brain in Mind, Learning Smarter, Different Brains Different Learners, The Great Memory Book, Teaching with the Brain in Mind, Brain-Compatible Strategies, Sizzle and Substance, Trainer's Bonanza, Tools for Engagement*, and *Super Teaching*. He's listed in Who's Who Worldwide and remains deeply committed to making a positive, significant and lasting difference in the way the world learns. Jensen is a sought-after conference speaker who consults and trains educators in the U. S. and abroad. The author can be contacted at eric@jlcbrain.com.

FREE to You...

For a FREE catalog of brain-compatible learning resources, call The Brain Store® at (800) 325-4769 or (858) 546-7555 or visit **www.thebrainstore.com** and browse our online catalog.

Learning Brain Expo®: **An Amazing 3-Day Brain/Mind Conference** Contact The Brain Store® at the numbers listed above or visit **www.brainexpo.com** for registration and session information.

Read a **FREE** issue of **Staff Developer: UPDATE**, an online publication of The Brain Store News Service™. Each monthly issue represents more than 100 hours of research on the most recent neuroscientific discoveries. Topics include: Environment • Active Learning • Presentation Strategies • Music and the Arts • Learning and Memory, and • The Social Brain. Fully cited articles are conveniently available right at your fingertips—only one mouse-click away! Receive hundreds of practical, brain-compatible teaching and training tips. Visit us online at **www.thebrainstore.com/news** and download your **FREE** issue!

Index